Screening History

The William E. Massey Sr.
Lectures in the History of
American Civilization
1991

Screening History

≈

GORE VIDAL

HARVARD UNIVERSITY PRESS
Cambridge, Massachusetts

This book is printed on acid-free paper, and its binding materials have been chosen
for strength and durability.

Library of Congress Cataloging-in-Publication Data

Vidal, Gore, 1925–
    Screening history / Gore Vidal.
        p.   cm.
        ISBN 0-674-79586-5 (alk. paper)
        1. Historical films—History and criticism.   2. Motion pictures—
Philosophy.   3. Motion pictures—Miscellanea.   I. Title.
PN1995.9.H5V54   1992
791.43'658—dc20   92-2912
                         CIP

Contents

Illustrations

Unless otherwise indicated, all photographs are from the author's private collection.

Page xii:
My father, Gene Vidal, explaining to me how to take off and land the prototype Hammond Y-1 airplane (May 13, 1936, Washington DC). Reproduced by permission of Sherman Grinberg Film Libraries, Inc.

Page 9:
My grandfather, Thomas Pryor Gore, and I.

Page 10:
Nina Gore Vidal Auchincloss Olds.

Page 14:
My father and I in the Hammond Y-1. Reproduced by permission of Sherman Grinberg Film Libraries, Inc.

Page 28:
The Prince and the Pauper: the moment in the woods when the Prince realizes that he is about to be killed. Photograph courtesy of the British Film Institute. © 1937 Turner Enterprises Co. All Rights Reserved. Reproduced by permission.

Page 30:
Franklin Delano Roosevelt, Eugene L. Vidal, and Henry A. Wallace, at Warm Springs, Georgia, a month or so after the November election of 1932.

Illustrations
≈

Page 36:
Gene Vidal in "The March of Time," circa 1935.

Page 45:
Flora Robson as Gloriana in *Fire Over England*. Photograph courtesy of the British Film Institute. Reproduced by permission of the Rohauer Collection.

Page 46:
Lord Burleigh explaining where England is in *Fire Over England*. Photograph courtesy of the British Film Institute. Reproduced by permission of the Rohauer Collection.

Page 47:
Vivien Leigh and Laurence Olivier in *That Hamilton Woman*. Photograph courtesy of the British Film Institute. © MCMXLI by Alexander Korda Films, Inc. Reproduced by permission of the Korda Collection, Central Television Enterprises Limited, and The Samuel Goldwyn Company.

Page 64:
Henry Fonda in the last frame of *The Young Mr. Lincoln*. Photograph courtesy of the British Film Institute. © 1939 by Twentieth Century Fox Film Corporation. Reproduced by permission.

Page 73:
Warrant Officer (Junior Grade) Eugene Luther Gore Vidal, First Mate of the Army Freight Supply Ship 35.

Page 75:
Amid Alaskan, if not "Alaskan," snow.

Page 77:
William Shatner and Inger Stevens as my grandparents in the television play *The Indestructible Mr. Gore*. Courtesy of the Wisconsin Center for Film and Theater Research.

Illustrations

≈

Page 97:
Boris Karloff as *The Mummy*. Photograph courtesy of the British Film Institute. Copyright © by Universal City Studios, Inc. Reproduced by permission of MCA Publishing Rights, a Division of MCA, Inc.

Following Page 52:
My life-long role model, Mickey Rooney, as Puck in MGM's *A Midsummer Night's Dream*. Photograph courtesy of the British Film Institute. © 1935 Turner Entertainment Co. All Rights Reserved. Reproduced by permission.

Mickey Rooney in *A Midsummer Night's Dream*. Photograph courtesy of the British Film Institute. © 1935 Turner Entertainment Co. All Rights Reserved. Reproduced by permission.

Bramwell Fletcher in *The Mummy*. Photograph courtesy of the British Film Institute. Copyright © by Universal City Studios, Inc. Reproduced by permission of MCA Publishing Rights, a Division of MCA, Inc.

Bobby and Billy Mauch in *The Prince and the Pauper*. Photograph courtesy of the British Film Institute. © 1937 Turner Enterprises Co. All Rights Reserved. Reproduced by permission.

The coronation scene in *The Prince and the Pauper*. Photograph courtesy of the British Film Institute. © 1937 Turner Enterprises Co. All Rights Reserved. Reproduced by permission.

Nelson's last words in *That Hamilton Woman*. Photograph courtesy of the British Film Institute. © MCMXLI by Alexander Korda Films, Inc. Reproduced by permission of the Korda Collection, Central Television Enterprises Limited, and The Samuel Goldwyn Company.

The young Olivier and Leigh in *Fire Over England*. Photograph courtesy of the British Film Institute. Reproduced by permission of the Rohauer Collection.

Illustrations
≈

Raymond Massey as Philip of Spain in *Fire Over England*. Photograph courtesy of the British Film Institute. Reproduced by permission of the Rohauer Collection.

Screening History

May 13, 1936, Washington DC. My father, Gene Vidal, is explaining to me how to take off and land the prototype Hammond Y-1, a plane so simple to operate that even, his words, "a ten-year-old could fly it." During the actual flight, my father wisely stayed on the ground with the Pathé newsreel crew while behind me crouched his administrative assistant, who knew even less about flying than I did. We survived. My father's dream for every American to own a "flivver plane" did not.

The Prince and the Pauper

≈

As I now move, graciously, I hope, toward the door marked Exit, it occurs to me that the only thing I ever really liked to do was go to the movies. Naturally, Sex and Art always took precedence over the cinema. Unfortunately, neither ever proved to be as dependable as the filtering of present light through that moving strip of celluloid which projects past images and voices onto a screen. Thus, in a seemingly simple process, screening history.

As a writer and political activist, I have accumulated a number of cloudy trophies in my melancholy luggage. Some real, some imagined. Some acquired from life, such as it is; some from movies, such as they are. Sometimes, in time, where we are as well as were, it is not easy to tell the two apart. Do I wake or sleep? For instance, I often believe that I served at least one term as governor of Alaska; yet written histories do not confirm this belief. No matter. Those were happy days, and who cares if they were real or not?

Not long ago George McGovern complained to me that he was having trouble getting lecture dates as he was no longer known to the rising generation despite his long senatorship and presidential candidacy. Briskly, I solved his problem. Tell the lecture bureau that you are a *former* president. As an ex-president, your lecture fees will go up. Since only a few of us here

1

in the United States of Amnesia actually know that you were *not* elected president in 1972, we will pledge ourselves to keep your secret. I fear that George did not fall apart with incontinent laughter. But then he still believes that there is an Alaska, while to me that balmy tropical state, with its baroque capital, Duluth, is so much dream-stuff and ever-changing. Do I speak now of art, perhaps? Perhaps.

I was born October 3, 1925, on the twenty-fifth birthday of Thomas Wolfe, the novelist. I have lived through two thirds of the twentieth century, and one third of the history of the United States of America. What has been your impression thus far, Mr. Vidal? as eager interviewers are wont to ask. *Well*, it could have been worse, I begin. Then the Japanese recording machine goes on the blink and while the interviewer tries to fix it, he asks me to tell him, off the record, what is Madonna really like? As I have never met her, I tell him.

It is a universal phenomenon that whether one is at Harvard or at Oxford or at the University of Bologna, after the dutiful striking of attitudes on subjects of professional interest, like semiology, the ice does not break until someone mentions the movies. Suddenly, everyone is alert and adept. There is real passion as we speak of the falling-off of Fellini in recent years, or of Madonna's curious contours and have they yet passed the once-disputed border of mere androgyny to some entirely new sexual continuum? Movies are the lingua franca of the twentieth century. The Tenth Muse, as they call the movies in Italy, has driven the other nine right off Olympus—or off the peak, anyway.

Recently I observed to a passing tape recorder that I was once a famous novelist. When assured, politely, that I was still known and read, I explained myself. I was speaking, I said, not of me but of a category to which I once belonged that now no longer exists. *I* am still here but my category is not. To

2

speak today of a famous novelist is like speaking of a famous cabinetmaker or speedboat designer. Adjective is inappropriate to noun. How can a novelist be famous, no matter how well known he may be personally to the press, when the novel itself is of no consequence to the civilized, much less to the generality? The novel as teaching aid is something else, but hardly famous.

There is no such thing as a famous novelist now, any more than there is such a thing as a famous poet. I use the adjective in the strict sense. According to authority, to be famous is to be much talked about, usually in a favorable way. It is as bleak and inglorious as that. Yet thirty years ago, novels were actually read and discussed by those who did not write them or, indeed, read them. A book *could* be famous then. Today the public seldom mentions a book, though people will often chatter about the screened versions of unread novels.

Contrary to what many believe, literary fame has nothing to do with excellence or true glory or even with a writer's position in the syllabus of a university's English Department, itself as remote to the Agora as Academe's shadowy walk. For any artist, fame is the extent to which the Agora finds interesting his latest work. If what he has written is known only to a few other practitioners, or to enthusiasts (Faulkner compared lovers of literature to dog breeders, few in number but passionate to the point of madness on the subject of blood lines), then the artist is not only not famous, he is irrelevant to his time, the only time that he has; nor can he dream of eager readers in a later century, as Stendhal did. If novels and poems fail to interest the Agora today, by the year 2091 such artifacts will not exist at all except as objects of monkish interest. This is neither a good nor a bad thing. It is simply not a famous thing.

Optimists, like the late John Gardner, regarded the university as a great good place where literature would continue to be not only worshiped but created. Perhaps he was right, though I do not like the look of those fierce theoreticians currently hacking away at the olive trees of Academe while seeding the Cephisus River with significant algae, their effect on the sacred waters rather like that of an oil spill off the coast of my beloved Alaska. Can there be a famous literary theoretician? Alas, no. The Agora has no interest in parlor games, other than Contract Bridge when one of the players is Omar Sharif. Literary theory is a glass-bead game whose reward for the ludic player is the knowledge that once he masters it, he will be admired by his peers as ludicrous.

But I have lately been taken to task by an English teacher for my "intemperate" attacks on English Departments, which have, she noted ominously, cost me my place on the syllabus. So I shall now desist and, like Jonah, wait for that greatest of fishes to open wide his jaws and take me in. After all, if you miss one syllabus, there'll be another in the next decade.

The best of literary critics is V. S. Pritchett, now in his ninetieth year. I find fascinating his recent descriptions of what the world was like in his proletarian youth. Books were central to the Agora of 1914. Ordinary Londoners were steeped in literature, particularly Dickens. People saw themselves in literary terms, saw themselves as Dickensian types while Dickens himself, earlier, had mirrored the people in such a way that writer and Agora were, famously, joined; and each defined the other.

In London, Pritchett and I belong to the same club. One afternoon we were sitting in the bar when a green-faced bishop stretched out his gaitered leg and tripped up a rosy-faced mandarin from Whitehall. As the knight fell against the wall, the bishop roared, "Pelagian heretic!" I stared with wonder. Pritchett looked very pleased. "Never forget," he said, "Dickens was a highly realistic novelist."

The Prince and the Pauper
≈

Today, where literature was movies are. Whether or not the Tenth Muse does her act on a theater screen or within the cathode tube, there can be no other reality for us since reality does not begin to *mean* until it has been made art of. For the Agora, Art is now sight and sound; and the books are shut. In fact, reading of any kind is on the decline. Half the American people never read a newspaper. Half never vote for president —the same half?

In 1925, the year that I was born, *An American Tragedy, Arrowsmith, Manhattan Transfer,* and *The Great Gatsby* were published. A nice welcoming gift, I observed to the Three Wise Men from PEN who attended me in my cradle, a bureau drawer in Washington DC's Rock Creek Park. I shall be worthy! I proclaimed; shepherds quaked.

For a moment, back then, it did look as if Whitman's dream of that great audience which would in turn create great writers had come true. Today, of course, when it comes to literacy, the United States ranks number twenty-three in the world. I have no idea what our ranking was then, but though the popular culture was a predictable mix of jazz and the Charleston and Billy Sunday, we must have had, proportionately, more and better readers then than now; literature was a part of life, and characters from contemporary fiction, like Babbitt, entered the language, as they had done in Pritchett's youth and before. Our public educational system was also a good one. Certainly, the *McGuffey's Eclectic Readers* of my grandfather's day would now be considered intolerably highbrow.

True, the Tenth Muse was already installed atop Parnassus, but she was mute. Actually, the movies were not as popular in the twenties as they had been before the First World War. Even so, in the year of my birth, Chaplin's *The Gold Rush* was released, while in my second year there appeared not only De Mille's *The Ten Commandments* and, no doubt in the interest of symmetry, *Flesh and the Devil* with Greta Garbo; it was also in my second year that the Tenth Muse suddenly spoke those minatory words "You ain't heard nothin' yet." Thus, the moving *and* talking picture began.

I saw and heard my first movie in 1929. My father and mother were still unhappily married and so we went, a nuclear family melting down, to the movies in St. Louis, where my father was general manager of TAT, the first transcontinental airline, later to merge with what is now, as of this week anyway, TWA.

I am told that as I marched down the aisle, an actress on the screen asked another character a question, and I answered her, in a very loud voice. So, as the movies began to talk, I began to answer questions posed by two-dimensional fictional characters thirty times my size.

My life has paralleled, when not intersected, the entire history of the talking picture. Although I was a compulsive reader from the age of six, I was so besotted by movies that one Saturday in Washington DC, where I grew up, I saw five movies in a day. But where it once took time and effort and money to see five movies in a day, now, with television and video cassettes, the screen has come to the viewer and we are all home communicants.

I don't think anyone has ever found startling the notion that it is not *what* things are that matters so much as *how* they are perceived. We perceive sex, say, not as it demonstrably is but as we think it ought to be as carefully distorted for us by the churches and the schools, by the press and by—triumphantly—the movies, which are, finally, the only validation to which that dull anterior world, reality, must submit.

The screening by CNN of our latest war was carefully directed by those who were producing the war. What this particular movie was all about is still not clear to us, nor are we ever apt to know what really happened until someone makes a back-stage movie like *The Bad and the Beautiful* or, perhaps, a *Platoon in the Desert*, a bitter, powerful film, quite as unrealistic, in its way, as the CNN–Pentagon release.

In February 1991 history was being invented before our eyes. From day to day we saw the editing and dubbing process at work. But we were merely viewers, while the actors on screen were also, in an eerie way, passive: part of a process no one seemed to be in control of. Even the Orson Welles *de nos jours*, the magnificent Herman Norman Schwarzkopf, was finally no more than a thousand points of pulsing light in a cathode ray . . .

Suddenly, the mood of prophecy is upon me! We shall yet be invited by the sponsors of USA, Inc., to bear witness to a presidential election in which the hero of the Gulf confronts the politically ambitious Terminator. It will be Schwarzkopf versus Schwarzenegger, the ultimate screen version of my old movie *The Best Man*, whose title was, of course, ironic . . .

I was struck by Eudora Welty's contribution to this series, published as *One Writer's Beginnings*. I have not her courage when it comes to speaking of my own life. I have also never been my own subject. But I do like the way that she set *her* scene, in Jackson, Mississippi, where her life and her life as a writer began. She starts, as everyone must, with a family. I could do the same, but do I dare? Contrary to legend, I was born of mortal woman, and if Zeus sired me, there is no record on file in the Cadet Hospital at West Point. But if I was usually born, there my resemblance to other writers ends. My mother did not shop; and my father was not cold and aloof, nor was he addicted to the sports page of the newspapers. Unlike most American fathers—sons, too—he did not live vicariously. He was his own hero, and the Agora had loved him for a time. He had been an All-American football player at West Point, and he had represented the United States in the decathlon at the Olympic Games. Later, he started three airlines. He was, I like to believe, the first person to realize that there was absolutely no point to cellophane.

"Dupont just invented this," he said, presenting me with a glassy cylinder. We unrolled the cellophane. "What's it for?" I asked. "Nothing!" He spoke with a true inventor's delight. For a season, in the thirties, one could see in the movie musicals cellophane used as curtains, tablecloths, showgirl dresses. Finally, cellophane, unlike celluloid, ended up as irrelevant wrapping. Yet it was nice in itself, like today's novel, say, or, as Cole Porter apostrophized in "You're the Top," "You're cellophane!"

Did my kindly maternal grandfather—from Mississippi, just like Eudora's—preside over a hardware business in Oklahoma City? No. From two unrelated accidents, he was blind at the age of ten. He put himself through law school, memorizing texts that were read to him by a cousin. At thirty-seven, having helped invent the state of Oklahoma—wit of this sort runs in our family—he became a famous senator.

Did my mother play bridge, bake pies in the kitchen, and perhaps drink too much of the cooking sherry? On the contrary, she was a flapper very like her coeval, Talullah Bankhead. (Faulkner went to his grave believing that coeval meant evil at the same time as.) In appearance she was a composite of Bette Davis and Joan Crawford. She never baked a pie, but she did manage to drink, in the course of a lifetime, the equivalent of the Chesapeake Bay in vodka. Eudora's people, just south of where the Gores lived, thought my mother fast. They were right. She married and divorced not only my famous father but a rich stockbroker; then she married a famous air force general, who promptly died. Meanwhile, the stockbroker married a woman whose daughter married a man who was elected

My grandfather, Thomas Pryor Gore (1870–1949), and I. At the same age that I am in the photograph, ten, he had been blinded by two separate accidents. The left eye is glass, and I used to play with it as he shaved. A man of wit and gravity, he was often undone by an eye that drifted to the northwest, rather like that of the comic Ben Turpin. First elected to the Senate in 1907, Gore was defeated in a primary shortly before this picture was taken in the summer of 1936. He is somber. "If there was any race other than the human race, I'd go join it."

president only to have his head shot off as the two of them were driving through Dallas on a hot November day. What is one to do, fictionally, with a family that has itself become a pervasive fiction that continues to divert the Agora?

I tried, once, to deal with my early days in a novel with no particular key but a number of what I still think to be

Nina Gore Vidal Auchincloss Olds (1903–1978). I cannot say that I ever liked my mother, but she had a rowdy flapperish charm. She became a Woman on the steps of the Capitol during Woodrow Wilson's Second Inauguration. She was wearing a brand-new green dress, she used to recall sadly. Was it thus the green twig bent?

cunning locks. It was called *Washington, DC*. I centered my narrative on the two houses where I grew up: That of Senator Gore in Rock Creek Park—now, significantly, the Malaysian Embassy—and that of my stepfather, the ill-named Merrywood, high above the Potomac River on the road to Manassas. Each house represented a different world that I would either have to master or be mastered by, the common fate of most children of Agora-noted families. All in all, I fancied this book. I was there and not there in the text. I had revealed and not revealed my peculiar family. I had also, without intending to, started on a history of the American Republic as experienced by one family and its emblematic connection to Aaron Burr.

During the next quarter-century I re-dreamed the republic's history, which I have always regarded as a family affair. But what was I to do with characters that were—are—not only famous but even preposterous? When my mother was asked why, after three famous marriages, she did not try for a fourth, she observed, "My first husband had three balls. My second, two. My third, one. Even *I* know enough not to press my luck."

At the time, *Washington, DC* was regarded as a novelized MGM movie, with sets by Cedric Gibbons and a part for Katharine Hepburn at her most mannered. So much for my strict realism. Eudora Welty may tell us all about *her* folks, and there is the pleasurable shock of recognition. But should I capture my family upon the page, the result is like a bad movie—or, worse, a good one. I never again used my own family as the stuff of fiction. We require no less than a Saint Simon. Unfortunately, we have received no more than a Kitty Kelley. What is the Agora trying to tell us?

It is possible that even when working from memory, I saw the world in movie terms, as who did not or, indeed, who does not? So let us examine the way in which one's perceptions of history were—and are—dominated by illustrated fictions of great power, particularly those screened in childhood.

Although most of the movie palaces of my Washington youth no longer exist, I can still see and smell them in memory. There was Keith's, across from the Treasury, a former vaudeville house where Woodrow Wilson used to go. Architecturally, Keith's was a bit too classically spacious for my taste. Also, the movies shown tended to be more stately than the ones to be seen around the corner in Fourteenth Street. Of course, no movie was ever truly dull, even the foreign ones shown at the Belasco in Lafayette Park, located, I believe, in the house of a fictional character of mine, known to history as William Seward, the purchaser of one of the Alaskas.

It was at the Belasco that I first saw myself screened in a Pathé newsreel. At the age of ten I took off and landed a plane. As Roosevelt's Director of Air Commerce, my father was eager to popularize a cheap, private plane that was, if not foolproof, childproof. Yet, thinking back, though he had grasped the silliness of cellophane, he seriously believed that since almost everyone could now afford a car, so almost everyone should be able to afford a plane. He dedicated years of his life to putting a cheap plane in every garage. Thanks to his dream, I, too, was famous for a summer. In a recent biography, I noted with amusement that one of the numerous lies that Truman Capote had told his childhood friend Harper Lee was that *he* had flown a plane at the age of ten.

Today anyone's life can be filmed from birth to death, thanks to the video camera. But for my generation there was no such immortality unless one were a movie star or a personage in the newsreels. Briefly, I was a newsreel personage. But what I really wanted to be was a movie star: specifically, I wanted to be Mickey Rooney, and to play Puck, as he had done in *A Midsummer Night's Dream*.

12

The Prince and the Pauper

≈

Parenthetically, life is always more ironic than art. While I was acting these lectures in Sanders Theater at Harvard (and revealing for the first time my envy of Mickey Rooney), Rooney was at the bookstore of the Harvard Coop, autographing copies of his latest book.

Last year I watched my famous flight for the first time since 1936. I am now old enough to be my father's father. He looks like the movie star. I don't. I am small, blond, with a retrousse nose as yet unfurled in all its Roman glory. I am to fly the plane, and a newsreel crew is on hand to record the event. My father was a master salesman: "This is your big chance to be a movie star," he had. "All you have to do is remember to take off into the wind." As I had flown the plane before, I am unafraid. I swagger down the runway, crawl into the plane, and pretend to listen to my father's instructions. But my eyes are not on him; they are on the cobra-camera's magic lens. Then I take the plane off; fly it; land with a bump; open the door; and face my interviewer.

"What fools these mortals be," Mickey's speech, as Puck, is sounding in my ears as I start to speak but cannot speak. I stare dumbly at the camera. My father fills in; then he turns to me. He cues me. What was it like, flying the plane? I remember the answer that he wants me to make: it was as easy as riding a bicycle. But, I had argued, it was a lot more complicated than riding a bicycle. Anyway, I am trapped in the wrong script. I say the line. Then I make a face to show my disapproval and, for an instant, I resemble not Mickey Rooney but Peter Lorre in *M*. My screen test has failed.

In 1935 I had seen Max Reinhardt's film, *A Midsummer Night's Dream*. Bewitched, I read the play, guessing at half the words; then, addicted to this strange new language, I managed to read all of Shakespeare before I was sixteen. (Yes, *Cymbeline*, too.) I am sure that my response was not unique. Certainly, other children must have gone to Shakespeare's text if only in search of Mickey and that Athenian forest where, after sunset, Oberon and Titania ride, attended by all sorts of mythical creatures; and those mortals who stray amongst them are subject to change. Metamorphosis, not entropy, is sovereign in these woods, and to this day I can still, in reverie, transport myself, to A Wood Near Athens on that midsummer's night before the Athenian Duke's marriage to the Amazon Queen.

Washington's principal movie palaces were on the east side of Fourteenth Street. The Capitol was the grandest, with a stage show and an orchestra leader called Sam Jack Kaufman, whom I once saw in the drugstore next to the theater. He wore an orange polo coat that matched his orange hair. He bought

As you can see, I am only interested in the camera that would, presently, make me a movie star like Mickey Rooney and the Mauch twins.

14

a cigar. Between each movie showing, there was an elaborate
stage show. I remember Peter Lorre's hair-raising and ear-
deafening impersonation of himself in *M*. Then, there were
The Living Statues. Well-known historic tableaux were enacted
by actors and actresses in white leotards. As people were
plumper then than now, sex could often be determined only
by wig. Even so, the effect was awesome in its marble-like
stillness. Boys in puberty, or older, affected lust when they saw
these figures, but those of us who were pre-pubescent sternly
looked only to the beauty and verisimilitude of the composi-
tions. Thus, in many a youthful bosom, a Ruskin—or even a
Rose Latouche—was awakened.

The Metropolitan was my favorite of the small theaters. I
think it was here that Warner Brothers pictures played. The
atmosphere was raffish. And the gum beneath the seats was
always fresh Dentyne, a flavor new that year. The Palace Theater was also congenial, while the Translux, devoted to newsreels and documentaries, was the only movie house to open in
my time, and its supermodern art deco interior smelled, for
some reason, of honey. At the time of the coronation of
George VI, there was displayed in the lobby a miniature royal
coach and horses. I wanted that coach more than I have ever
wanted anything. But my father made an insufficient offer to
the manager of the theater. Later, I acquired the coach through
my stepfather, to add to a collection of three thousand soldiers
kept in the attic at Merrywood. Here I enacted an endless series
of dramas, all composed by me. If ever there was a trigger to
the imagination, it was those lead soldiers. Today they would
be proscribed because war is bad and women under-represented
in their ranks. But I deployed my troops for other purposes
than dull battle. I was my own Walter Scott. I was also the
Warner Brothers, too, and Paramount—paramount, too, as I
played *auteur*, so like God, we have been told by film critics.

The most curious of the movie houses of my childhood

15

was The Blue Hen at Rehoboth Beach, Delaware, where the family went occasionally in the summer. What a Blue Hen had to do with a movie house I puzzled over for a half century until a young Delawarean in Sanders Theater told me that the Blue Hen was the state university mascot.

At the Blue Hen I saw *Love Song of the Nile* with Ramon Navarro and Helen Broderick: a film that I can find no record of anywhere except in my memory. But I do know that Egypt was on my mind as early as 1932 when I saw *The Mummy*, with Boris Karloff. The effect of that film proved to be life-long. Also, it must be recalled that in those days if you saw a movie once, that was that. The odds were slim that you would ever see it again. There were no Museums of Modern Art or film retrospectives. Today, thanks to video cassettes, one can see a film as often as one likes. But since we knew that we would have only the one encounter, we learned how to concentrate totally.

In a sense, learning a film at a single screening must have been something like a return to that oral tradition where one acquired a Homeric song through aural memory. In any case, at seven I confronted not the rage of Achilles but the obsession of a man three thousand years dead. I was never to forget my first sight of the mummy in its case as, nearby, an archaeologist reads a spell from an ancient papyrus. Slowly, the linen-wrapped hand moves. The archaeologist turns; sees what we cannot see; starts to laugh, and cannot stop laughing. He has gone mad.

Fifty-eight years later, I watched the movie for the first time since its release and I became, suddenly, seven years old again, mouth ajar, as I inhabited, simultaneously, both ancient Egypt and pre-imperial Washington DC. Then, as the film ended, my seven-year-old world dissolved, to be glimpsed no more except for the odd background shot of a city street, say, in a 1932 movie, where now-dead people are very much alive, unconscious of the screening camera as they go about their business, in the margins of a film where they are forever, briefly, alive.

What appeals in *The Mummy*, other than the charnel horror? Obviously, any confirmation that life continues after death has an appeal to almost everyone except enlightened Buddhists. No one wants to be extinct. Hence, the perennial popularity of ghost stories or movies about visits to heaven that prove to be premature since heaven can always wait, even if hell be here.

For a time, after *The Mummy*, I wanted to become an archaeologist, though not like the one played by Bramwell Fletcher, whose maniacal laughter still haunts me. (Years later, Fletcher acted in the first play that I wrote for live television.) I preferred the other archaeologist in the film, as performed by David Manners, who also appeared in *Roman Scandals* (1933), another film that opened for me that door to the past where I have spent so much of my life-long present.

From earliest days, the movies have been screening history, and if one saw enough movies, one learned quite a lot of simple-minded history. Stephen Runciman and I met on an equal basis not because of my book *Julian*, which he had written about, but because I knew *his* field, thanks to a profound study of Cecil B. De Mille's *The Crusades* (1935), in which Berengaria, as played by Loretta Young, turns to her Lionheart husband and pleads, "Richard, you *gotta* save Christianity." A sentiment that I applauded at the time but came later to deplore.

Thanks to *A Tale of Two Cities*, *The Scarlet Pimpernel*, and *Marie Antoinette*, my generation of pre-pubescents understood at the deepest level the roots—the flowers, too—of the French Revolution. Unlike Dickens' readers, we *knew* what the principals looked and sounded like. We had been there with them.

In retrospect, it is curious how much history *was* screened in those days. Today, Europe still does stately tributes to the Renaissance, usually for television; otherwise, today's films are stories of him and her and now, not to mention daydreams of unlimited shopping with credit cards. Fortunately, with time even the most contemporary movie undergoes metamorphosis, *becomes* history as we get to see real life as it was when the film was made, true history glimpsed through the window of a then-new, now-vintage, car.

My first and most vivid movie-going phase was from 1932 to 1939—from seven to fourteen. Films watched before puberty are still the most vivid. *A Midsummer Night's Dream*, *The Mummy*, *Roman Scandals*, *The Last Days of Pompeii*. Ancient Egypt, Classical Rome, Shakespeare when he was still in thrall to that most magical of poets, Ovid.

Then there is something called *The Mystery of the Blue Room*, of which I can find no trace in reference books or even in my memory except that one character was called Irene. I promptly wrote a story called "The Mystery of the Blue Room," which I read aloud to the family. My character, called Irene, likes to ask people questions that they have already answered because, as I pointed out, she never listens to what anyone says. This was plainly a reference to my wool-gathering grandmother. In real life, I have never set foot in a blue room except the downstairs oval drawing room at the White House where, inspired no doubt by the unmistakably blue walls, I solved for an Attorney General the mystery of his bad character.

Although *Roman Scandals* was a comedy, starring the vaudevillian Eddie Cantor, I was told not to see it. I now realize why the movie, which I saw anyway, had been proscribed. The year of release was 1933. The country was in an economic depression. Drought was turning to dust the heart of the country's farm land, and at the heart of the heart of the dust bowl was my grandfather's state of Oklahoma. So bad was the drought that many of his constituents were abandoning their farms and moving west to California. The fact that so many Oklahomans, Okies for short, were obliged to leave home was a very sore point with their senator.

At the beginning of *Roman Scandals* we see the jobless in Oklahoma. One of them is Eddie Cantor, who is knocked on the head and transported to ancient Rome, much as Dorothy was taken by whirlwind from Kansas to Oz; thus, a grim Oklahoma is metamorphosed into a comic-strip Rome.

My memory of the Depression is more of talk on the radio and in the house than of actual scenes of apple-selling in the street. Also, I did not always understand what I heard. When stockmarket shares fell, I thought that chairs were falling out of second-story windows. I did know that senators spent their days in the Senate chamber passing bills—dollar bills, I thought, from one to another, by no means an entirely surreal image.

At the age of five I sat in the Senate gallery and watched as T. P. Gore was sworn in for a fourth term. Defeated in 1920, he had made a triumphant return in 1930. I recall the skylit pale greens of the chamber so like the aquarium in the basement of the Commerce Building. I was also very much aware of my grandfather's enemy (and my father's friend and employer), the loudly menacing Franklin D. Roosevelt, with a black spot—like a dog's—over his left eyebrow. He was always in the papers and on radio; worse, there he was in practically every newsreel, smiling balefully at us and tossing his huge head about.

Finally, in the spring of 1932, I saw at first hand history *before* it was screened. A thousand veterans of the First War had arrived in the capital to demand a bonus for their services in the late and, to my grandfather, unnecessary war. These

19

The Prince and the Pauper

≈

Until my mother married a second time, there was no fortune in the family. Cunningly, my father managed to lose control of each of the airlines that he had founded; but then he had no interest in money, only in the making of new things. Senator Gore lived on his salary as a senator, $15,000 a year. He was also the first and, I believe, last senator from an oil state to die without a fortune. But though we were relatively poor, I could tell that I was not like the other children because of the questions that my teachers would ask me about my father and grandfather, and was it true what the papers said?

When I asked my grandparents about the newspapers, they replied in unison, "If you read it in the papers, it isn't true." But then populists have never had a good press in Freedom's Land. I was also warned never to answer the questions of strangers, and, of course, I always did. To one reporter, I said that my stepfather could not possibly have been the father of my half-sister as he had not known my mother long enough. Although I had no inkling of the facts of life, I had an instinct for the telling detail. Later, at school, when asked what my father did, I said, "He's in the newspapers," which seemed to me a precise way of accounting for his activities as Director of Air Commerce.

In 1936 I moved from Rock Creek Park to the house, Merrywood, across the Potomac, and money suddenly hedged us all round. At the height of the Depression there were five servants in the house, *white servants*, a sign of wealth unique for Washington in those years. My stepfather was an heir to Standard Oil, the nemesis of T. P. Gore and Huey Long. Although I now lived the life of a very rich prince, I was still *un*conscious of class differences other than the relation between black and white, which was something as fixed in our city then as the Capitol dome, and as unremarkable. But the rock that had landed between my grandfather and me in the back of the car was a sharp and unmistakable signal that there were others who were not, indeed, princes at all; that there were millions of people to whom an old-fashioned word applied—pauper.

I recently watched *The Prince and the Pauper*, a Warner Brothers movie I had not seen since 1937. Although something of an avatar of Mark Twain, I have never read the novel on which the film was based. I suppose that the movie's effect on my conscious and unconscious self was so great that I feared further stimulus, or disillusion.

Like most of the movies that impress themselves on a child, the story is simple but the subtexts are disturbingly complex if one is the right age to be affected by them. The prince and the pauper were played by Bobby and Billy Mauch, identical twins who were the same age as I, twelve. So there was I, in surrogate, on the screen not once but twice, not only prince but pauper, and the two of us were so alike as to be interchangeable as well.

I do not know if a desire to be a twin is a common one, or if such a longing might run in families, psychically as well as genetically. My grandmother Gore lost her twin at birth, and it required no uncanny knowledge of the human heart for the family to figure out that when she took over the task of being not only wife but eyes to her husband, she had found in him her long-lost twin. On the other hand, I was quite pleased to be an only child. Later, I acquired various step- and half-brothers and sisters, but I never really knew any of them, as I was gone for good at seventeen—into the army and to all those other worlds elsewhere.

When I watched *The Prince and the Pauper* the first time, I wanted to be not one but two. Lonely children often have imaginary playmates but I was never lonely; rather, I was solitary, and wanted no company at all other than books and movies, and my own imagination. I was Puck; I was a long-dead Egyptian; I was a time traveler to Rome; I was many other selves. But now, suddenly, I wanted to be not Puck, or even Mickey Rooney. I wanted to be myself, twice. I do not dare speculate upon what the school of Vienna—I refer, of course, to the Riding School—would make of this. But I don't think that my response to the film was unusual, particularly if one were the actors' age and so could easily identify with the notion of the two as really one and that one oneself, or with the general proposition that a palpable duplicate of oneself would be the ideal companion.

A current pejorative adjective is narcissistic. Generally, a narcissist is anyone better-looking than you are, but lately the adjective is often applied to those "liberals" who prefer to improve the lives of others rather than exploit them. Apparently, a concern for others is self-love at its least attractive, while greed is now a sign of the highest altruism. But then to reverse, periodically, the meanings of words is a very small price to pay for the freedom not only to conform but to consume.

The childhood desire to be a twin does not seem to me to be narcissistic in the vulgar Freudian sense. After all, one is oneself; and the other other. It is the sort of likeness that makes for wholeness, and is it not that search for likeness, that desire and pursuit of the whole—as Plato has Aristophanes remark— that is the basis of all love? As no one has ever actually found wholeness in another human being, no matter of what sex, the twin is the closest that one can ever come toward wholeness with another; and, dare one invoke biology and the origin of our species, there is always, back of us mammals, doomed to die once we have procreated, our sexless ancestor the amoeba, which never dies as it does not reproduce sexually but merely —serenely?—breaks in two and identically replicates.

Anyway, I thought Billy and Bobby Mauch were cute as a pair of bug's ears, and I wished I were either one of them, *one* of them, mind you. I certainly did not want to be two of *me*, as one seemed more than enough to go around even in a famous family. Yet doubleness has always fascinated me, as mirrors do, as filmed images do. I have read that a recurring theme in my work is doubleness or duplicity. If this is the case, I see now where it might have—consciously at least—begun.

Errol Flynn was the star of *The Prince and the Pauper*; he was a swashbuckling actor at the height of his beauty if not fame. He befriends the pauper and then, when prince and pauper change clothes and places, Flynn befriends the prince, thinking he is the pauper, until at last he is convinced that there are indeed two boys and that the prince is in danger. The plot, as I recap it, is pure Shakespeare. It is also impure Samuel Clemens—or is he by now entirely Mark Twain? Certainly, he was obsessed by twins, and by the likeness of one to another. But then what does his pen name mean, if it does not mean two or twain or twin? I often wonder what I might have become if they had filmed not *The Prince and the Pauper* but that blackest of American "twin" fables, *Puddin'head Wilson*.

Although Errol Flynn is charming as an ideal older brother, I had completely forgotten that he was in the movie. Plainly, I didn't want an older brother. I was fixated on the twins themselves. On the changing of clothes, and the reversal of roles. On the descent of the boy prince into the life of the poor, which struck many bells for someone who had actually seen the Boners plain. We now know, through such FBI informers as Ronald Reagan, that in the thirties and the forties Hollywood was being infiltrated by the Reds and that writers in the pay of Moscow were subtly poisoning every script that they could with malicious attacks on greed and selfishness and those other traits that have made our country great. It is true, of course, that some of the movie writers *were* Communists but, as they all agreed in later years, you couldn't get anything of a political nature into any film. This has also been true in my experience.

On the other hand, it is worth at least a doctoral thesis for some scholar to count how often in films of the thirties and forties a portrait of Franklin Roosevelt can be found, usually hanging on a post-office wall; and then try to discover who put it there: the writer, the director, the producer—the set designer?

At a subconscious level, there was actually a good deal of politics in even the simplest of everyday stories, while historical pieces could always conceal messages, since studios were certain that nothing that happened *then* could ever have anything at all to do with *now*. For me, at twelve, the poor of London in their encampment, Robbers' Roost, were just like the Boners in the Anacostia Flats.

The film's overt political message is straightforward: a good king will listen to the people and help them. Oddly enough, kings with absolute power were a staple of American movies. One seldom saw democracy in action, and when one did the results were apt to be simple-minded fables like those of Frank Capra.

More is to be learned, I believe, from William Keighley, *auteur de The Prince and the Pauper* as well as of *Babbitt*, than from Capra. The prince's father, Henry VIII, explains to his son the nature of power. Why the Warner Brothers thought that the American public would find interesting a disquisition on princely power in Renaissance times is a secret that Jack L. Warner took to his grave. On the other hand, the king's musings were possibly addressed to the serfs at Warner Brothers, a studio known for its love of tradition, particularly the annual Christmas layoff.

The king confides: "Never trust so much, love so much, need anyone so much that you cannot betray them with a smile." This is true Machiavelli, and must have seemed startling to an audience imbued with such Christian values as turning the other cheek while meekly obeying your master. But I am now convinced that my generation of Americans either went to church *or* to the movies for spiritual guidance. As a third-generation atheist, I was nourished by the screen, and I was particularly struck by the king's sermon, so like my grand-father's bleak wisdom. "In politics you must always treat an enemy as if he might one day be a friend, and a friend as if he might one day be an enemy." My grandfather did concede that he found the second part hard to do, but that did not make it any the less advisable.

The scene that I remembered best was a forest at night, much like A Wood Near Athens. The prince has been taken captive. He is told that he is to be killed right then and there with a knife. The lighting is beautiful, and if Ted Turner and Jane ever decide to paint this black-and-white film, I hope they will use Gainsborough's delicate earth colors.

There is a startling close-shot of the prince's face as he realizes that he is about to die. Then, invited to pray, he gets off a bold line: he hopes that his father is *not* watching from Heaven because the king would be ashamed of the treacherous Englishman, but not of his son. I still feel the force of this scene. For the first time, the boy knows that he is about to stop being. Like most children, I often used to imagine what death must be like. But unlike most, I had no belief, or even interest, in an afterlife. To me, if not the prince, death is *not* being; and that is why for us who know only being, death is literally unimaginable, try as hard as one might to imagine—what? An empty room where one is not? Put out the light and then put out the light? For the young, death is supremely unnatural. For the old, it is so natural that it is not worth thinking about.

As I had never for an instant believed in an afterlife, I suppose that all I could come up with, at twelve, was the formulation that as one was not before birth, one will not be

27

This is the moment in the woods when the Prince realizes that he is about to be killed. I have never lost—on the inner tape, as it were, of memory—this image of mortality.

after death, and so there you are, or not, as the case may be. For some, the notion of images impressed on celluloid provides a spurious sense of immortality, as does, indeed, the notion that those light-rays which record our images will keep on bending about the universe forever. There are those who find comfort in such concepts. I don't.

Errol Flynn saves the prince in the wood, and as the pauper is about to be crowned king, the true prince is restored, and all is right with a world where a good boy-king will stand up to evil, whether played by Claude Rains or by Hitler.

So, in a single film, screened at the susceptible time of puberty, one experienced the shock, as it were, of twinship.

Also, the knowledge of how to exercise power. Also, the contrast between rich and poor that even I had been made aware of as the Depression deepened, and there was no help on earth for the poor except from the king, if he be good and well-informed. This was much the attitude of the American people at that time to their sovereigns, Franklin and Eleanor, who were opposed, as was the good prince, by evil lords. Finally, there is the impact of imminent death upon a twelve-year-old. Of all the facts of life, death is the oddest. Suddenly, there it is, in a moonlit forest, at the hand of a traitor with a knife; and then no more life. No anything. Nothing.

Underlying the film, there is an appeal to altruism. Now altruism is a brief phase through which some adolescents must pass. It is rather like acne. Happily, like acne, only a few are permanently scarred. Yet the prince in the film is obliged to note that there are others in the world beside himself (not to mention a pauper duplicate), and to those others he must be responsible. This is a highly un-American point of view but not without its charm for the youthful viewer, who will discover for himself, more soon than late, that one must always put oneself first, except when the American empire requires a war and then, *Dulce et decorum est pro patria mori*. I believe that my generation of Americans was the very last even to begin to take seriously that once-powerful invocation.

But now the feature film's over. The newsreel begins. The Japanese sink an American gunboat on a river in China. Senator Gore is defeated for a fifth term. "All is lost," he declares, "including honor." The House Un-American Activities Committee is formed. The Director of Air Commerce resigns. The Munich Agreement is signed. Hitler takes over Czechoslovakia's Sudetenland.

Next: Previews of Coming Attractions. And coming to this theater is—what else?—*Fire Over England*, yet again.

Franklin Delano Roosevelt, Eugene L. Vidal, and Henry A. Wallace. This photograph was taken at Warm Springs, Georgia, a month or so after the November election of 1932. My father has been summoned by the President-elect: Will he accept the Directorship of Air Commerce, a post that would be the equivalent of a European Minister of Aviation? My father served as Director for four turbulent years. Wallace has just accepted the secretaryship of Agriculture, while the President has just had a haircut; he is in a bad mood because the barber took too much off the sides.

Fire Over England

≋

In that most attractively adhesive of Russian novels, *Oblomov*, the protagonist devotes his life to finding more and better reasons for not getting out of bed. He finally stops going to the coffeehouse to see his friends because he knows that they will want to argue about the current situation in Turkey, and since none of them has ever been to Turkey, what they will discuss will be something the newspapers have made up and called Turkey. So why not stay home in bed and dream one's own Ottoman Empire?

From Gutenberg's machine to radio, history was prosed for us. Current history-in-the-making came to us, as did past history, through ink upon a page, and if the historian or journalist was sufficiently powerful in his deployment of words— Shakespeare as Tudor publicist, say—what we read often became more real to us than what we knew to be the case even when we had some firsthand knowledge of a written-about occasion. Radio caused a shift from eye to ear. The human voice dramatized as well as described, while music could be artfully added, producing *melo*-drama. Prosed history could do none of this without considerable imagination on the part of the reader, and good readers are almost as rare as good writers. Radio was a mechanical reversion to the world before the fifth century BC when poets and town criers sang the news, and no one read.

31

Fire Over England

≈

Movies changed our world forever. Henceforth, history would be screened; first, in meeting houses known as movie houses; then at home through television. As the whole world is more and more linked by satellites, the world's view of the world can be whatever a producer chooses to make it. I am stating all these obvious things because I may have given the impression that I was going to confine myself to those ninety-minute entertainments that were screened in the theaters of my youth. Actually, my subject is how, through ear and eye, we are both defined and manipulated by fictions of such potency that they are able to replace our own experience, often becoming our *sole* experience of a reality become as irreal as the Turkey of Oblomov's coffeehouse, or the Alaska of my dreams.

Certainly, no reality intrudes on our presidential elections. They are simply fast-moving fictions. Empty of content at a cognitive level but, at a visceral level, very powerful indeed, as the tragic election of Willie Horton to the governorship of Massachusetts demonstrated in 1988. But, for the moment, I shall revert to the pre-television world of my youth, and ponder how we were shaped by the movies that we saw then and why they were what they were, to the extent that I am able to decode them now.

As *The Prince and the Pauper* haunted my pre-pubescent years, so *Fire Over England*, and others of its kind, were to shape my adolescence. During my first twelve years, Depression and the threat of revolution dominated our screens, as they did our on-going history. The next seven years were dominated, first, by the seduction of the United States by England, a replay of 1914–1917; and then by the war itself.

As I was part of a political clan, located in the political capital of the United States, the debate over whether or not to take part, yet again, in a foreign war was particularly fierce.

Fire Over England
≈

For those who find disagreeable today's Zionist propaganda, I can only say that gallant little Israel of today must have learned a great deal from the gallant little Englanders of the 1930s. The English kept up a propaganda barrage that was to permeate our entire culture, with all sorts of unexpected results. Since the movies were by now the principal means of getting swiftly to the masses, Hollywood was subtly and not so subtly infiltrated by British propagandists.

In *The Loved One*, Evelyn Waugh has described Hollywood's British colony as it appeared to him immediately after the war. By then the great work was done, and the English actors and writers and directors, who had helped create a pro-British atmosphere in the country, were now able to relax and enjoy their slow games of cricket beneath the orange trees, not to mention beneath the maleficent gaze of Mr. Waugh. But a dozen years before Waugh's arrival, the British colony had been hard at work, giving the Americans a glorious view of the "mother country," as they liked to call it, a phrase calculated to put on edge my grandfather's Anglo-Irish false teeth, not to mention the real ones of my Romanischer father.

In the thirties—as in the teens—the country was divided over whether or not the United States should join England and France against Germany. But the division was not exactly right down the middle. I have not consulted any ancient poll, but it is my impression that something like two thirds of our people wanted to stay out of the European war. The so-called liberals—as they are always so-called—included Franklin Roosevelt. They were eager to go to war, once war came, on England's side. The so-called conservatives, like Senator Gore, were against war in general and any war to help the British Empire in particular. Today, when the meanings of so many words have been reversed, the conservatives speak fiercely against the, so-called by them, isolationists on the left, while

33

the left (also known as Paleolithic conservatives) speaks of minding our own business and restoring a wrecked polity, thanks to forty years of profitless—for the people at large—imperialism.

It had been hard enough for Wilson to maneuver us into the First War, as my grandfather believed that he had meant to do as early as 1916. We got nothing much out of that war except an all-out assault on the Bill of Rights in 1919 and, of course, the prohibition of alcohol. The world was not even made safe for democracy, a form of government quite alien to the residents of our alabaster cities, much less to those occupants of our fruited plains.

Meanwhile, a postwar depression had hit us. The black population was restive. For a few months in 1939, I kept a diary. In addition to faithfully recording the weather, I sternly noted the number of strikes that were ravaging the land. I shared, naturally, in that hatred of organized labor which has been the one political constant in my lifetime, culminating in Ronald Reagan's most popular gesture, the smashing of the air-controllers' union. No alternative view of organized labor has ever come to us through the popular media. If labor leaders were not crooks like Jimmy Hoffa, they were in the pay of Moscow. Meanwhile, ritually, communism and socialism were demonized though never actually explained. On the other hand, fascism was treated with some respect in the early thirties. After all, Hitler was against communism.

In 1935 Senator Gore predicted that the World War, fitfully hibernating since the Versailles treaty, would start up again. As the only member of the Senate to have served in the 1917 Senate, he was very much an ancestral voice, prophesying war while calling for nonintervention. The next year he was defeated for reelection with President Roosevelt's exuberant connivance.

Fire Over England

≈

On the other hand, my father was a West Point graduate. As Roosevelt's Director of Air Commerce, he had not only systematized American civil aviation but he had been given the secret job of procuring air bases for the coming war whose locus, for us, would not be Europe but the Pacific. For the better part of the century, we had been preparing for a military showdown with Japan.

In those days there was a monthly film documentary called "The March of Time"; it was produced by the publishers of the magazines *Time*, *Life*, and *Fortune*. Today's equivalent would be CBS's "Sixty Minutes." "The March of Time" screened the world through the imperial American eyes of Christ-loving, Red-fearing, people-hating Henry Luce, who had got some of the financing for the original *Time* magazine from his Yale classmate, my stepfather. I was obliged to call him Uncle Harry. The thick hair on the backs of his fingers made them look like caterpillars. I once heard him say to my mother that his famous wife, Clare Boothe Luce, did not understand him. I was thrilled: this was MGM dialogue at its best. Years later, he confided to me that the true mission of the United States in the world was the Christianization of China. Uncle Harry was mad as a hatter. But he was a master of the art of screening history.

I have spent the last year screening not only movies but newsreels from the 1930s and 40s, partly in preparation for these meditations, and partly to make sense to myself why we were what we were and why we did what we did; and to what extent we were shaped by the likes of Henry Luce, himself shaped by a missionary father in China.

As I can now see, "The March of Time" doted on *my* father. Aviation was glamorous and he was glamorous. He was only thirty-eight when he took over what was, in effect, the job of Secretary of Aviation. He was also, I now realize, a

35

conscious player in the pre-war war games. One "March of Time" is devoted to the story of how Gene Vidal took over an uninhabited Pacific island and turned it into a fueling base for an American trans-Pacific commercial air route. Unfortunately, the island was a part of the far-flung British Empire, and my father had forgotten to tell the British what he was up to.

CUT to exterior shot of barren island. CUT to my father, grinning. CUT to comic Englishman who says "His Majesty's government views with alarm . . ." CUT to my father at his desk in the Commerce Building. He is deeply sincere. He tells

"The March of Time," circa 1935. My father, Eugene Luther Vidal (1895–1969), is trying to explain how it was that he occupied—and converted into an American air base—a British island in the Pacific. The war with Japan was already under way, of course, six years before Pearl Harbor.

us that no one had ever told him that the island belonged to England, and that he couldn't be more sorry. He remembered looking at the map just before he took over the island, and he was pretty certain that it was not pink like the rest of the Empire. Maybe the cartographers were at fault . . .

In any case, we kept the island and it played a part in the long-awaited and planned-for war with Japan. A war of Ideas, as always. *We* had the idea that the Pacific Ocean should be ours; *they* thought it should be theirs. Plainly, two powerful ideologies on a collision course.

During the thirties, we had viewed with growing alarm Japan's annexation of Manchuria and Korea; then came the invasion of China and the sinking by the Japanese of an American gunboat in a Chinese river. This was almost the pretext that we needed for war. Unfortunately, we were not yet ready to fight. But Uncle Harry continued to remind the world that freedom-loving China was America's first line of defense, rather like Kurdistan today.

This was the political background to what was to be the most brilliant decade in the history of the movies, a decade that started with the Depression and ended when the war began. By 1945, with the defeat of Germany in the east and of Japan in the west, the American empire was at high noon, its emblem not the eagle but a death-seeding phallic cloud. *In hoc signes* was born what Uncle Harry called "the American century." Five years later the American century ended in Korean mud. Thanks to modern technology, as the thousand-year Reich had earlier discovered, history now comes equipped with a fast-forward button.

In the pre-war decade, I was as absorbed in politics as any grown-up. At the beginning of the fateful imperial decade Washington was a company town that made politics for the whole nation; at the end, for the whole world. It was in 1936 that I moved from my grandfather's house in Rock Creek Park, my true home, across the Potomac River to the house called Merrywood. My mother had become Mrs. Hugh D. Auchincloss, a ridiculous name, to my mind, usually mispronounced and spelled. Although Americans are as class-conscious as any other people, our rulers have never gone in for titles, on the ground that certain names or combinations of names will rank its possessor as precisely as any coronet. I fear that the strawberry leaves of Merrywood had the same effect on me as the poison ivy that also flourished on the Potomac palisades.

The worlds of my father and grandfather were to me the real ones. They did things, and the rich did not. They were famous, and the rich were not. Fortunately, I was sent off to boarding schools and so I was spared a good deal of family life of the sort that our generation saw, so sumptuously screened, in such movies as *The Philadelphia Story* and *Holiday*.

As I moved to Merrywood, Hitler moved into the Rhineland, and England was divided between those, like Chamberlain, who would appease the dictator in order to gain time and those, like Churchill, who were ready to fight, ready or not. The United States was now split between interventionists and isolationists. The interventionists were led by the East Coast gentry, with their banks and their web of connections with old Europe. The isolationists were populists in tandem with such Britain-haters as the Irish and the German hyphenates. During 1936 the lines were being carefully drawn, though few knew it at the time except, perhaps, newsreel addicts like myself.

In May of that year, I was screened; British Pathé nicely called me the "Boy Airman." Then came the abdication of Edward VIII, in order to marry the woman he loved, a tough cookie from nearby Baltimore. Every movie house everywhere excitedly screened the king's long crisis. Finally, at Merrywood, we gathered around the radio in my mother's art-deco bedroom to hear the king's farewell speech. We wept. Then came the coronation of George VI. We cheered. For the first time the ceremony in the Abbey was screened by the cameras, and all the world stood witness as the little idol was anointed and dressed up and became King-Emperor, a title that ravished me, for had I not lived on the screen the life of a Bengal Lancer two years before? and of Clive of India the year before that?

The title also ravished its former holder, the Duke of Windsor. Years later he told me that "when I was Prince of Wales, and traveling in India, if anybody had told me that all this would end in my lifetime, I'd have thought him crazy. Anyway," and the wizened face smiled, "I was the *last* King-Emperor. That is, to the end, you know?" Although the Duke of Windsor was of a stupidity more suitable to the pen of Wodehouse than of Shakespeare, he was to me forever glamorous because he had been artfully screened for me all my life, as had his family in the past and in the present so that, in time of peril, we Americans might honor and love them and their lovely kingdom from which we had, somehow, been sadly separated.

On our screens, in the thirties, it seemed as if the only country on earth was England and there were no great personages who were not English, or impersonated by English actors. I recall no popular films about Washington or Jefferson or Lincoln the president. For reasons I shall come to, our history was thought unsuitable for screening. As a result, England, and to a lesser extent, France, dominated all our dreams.

There were the ubiquitous newsreels of the new king and queen on coronation day, as well as feature films of gallant little England menaced by Spain's Armada and Napoleon's armies. There were also biographical films of Chatham and Pitt, of Clive and Disraeli, of Wellington and Nelson. It was not until 1939 that we got a part of our story, *Gone with the*

Wind. But by then a whole generation of us film-watchers had defended the frontiers of the Raj and charged with the Light Brigade at Balaklava. We served neither Lincoln nor Jefferson Davis; we served the Crown.

On screen, the French were not too far behind the British. We got rather a lot of the French Revolution, a dangerous subject, one would have thought, during the Depression. Fortunately, our sympathies were engaged not by the cake-spurning poor but by Marie Antoinette, gallantly portrayed by Norma Shearer, whose luminous wall-eye was never more effective than when she was about to lose her head, first, to Tyrone Power and then to the guillotine.

The Three Musketeers—confusingly four in number—transplanted us to the court of Louis XIII, a rather more satisfying place than that of the feckless Louis XVI, or even that of sardonic Louis XV, as played by John Barrymore. We were taken even further back in time to François Villon, played by the English romantic star Ronald Colman. Unknown to us at the time, Colman was British Intelligence's man in Hollywood, in place to make sure that England would look its best on the screen.

After abdication and coronation, every other film had an obligatory coronation scene of which the best, by far, was that in *The Prisoner of Zenda*, where Ronald Colman is a mittel-Europa monarch with an English look-alike (we are back now to twins): They exchange places, and so on. By 1937, royal-mania had gripped the great republic along with a tide of pro-British sentiment that came to a well-calculated crescendo in the spring of 1939 when the king and queen came to Washington on a state visit.

I stood in the crowd in front of the Treasury Building and cheered the monarch. George VI was a very small, thin man, with a delicate face painted nut-brown in marked contrast to the huge red face of our president, who kept tossing his head around and grinning in imitation of his wife's uncle, Theodore Roosevelt. But then presidents almost always imitate successful predecessors. As a speaker, Kennedy imitated Franklin Roosevelt, who imitated Woodrow Wilson, who in turn imitated . . . Jefferson Davis, it was once cruelly said. Now with a century of screened history available at the touch of a button, a wide range of prototypes are available to the ambitious politician.

On that memorable June day, the lords of Merrywood joined the other magnates in paying court to the king and queen at a garden party to which only a limited number of magnates were invited because, as the British ambassador remarked, "It's rather like the kingdom of heaven. Some are chosen and some are not." He took early retirement. But the newsreels of king and queen eating hot dogs at Hyde Park with Franklin and Eleanor caused many a heart to beat faster for England, while giving such patriots as my grandfather heartburn.

On both sides of the Atlantic the movies were preparing us for a wartime marriage with our English and French cousins, against our Italian and German cousins. Meanwhile, outside the newsreel theaters, Japan was almost entirely ignored. A series of detective stories featured a highly efficient and courteous Japanese spy called Mr. Moto; otherwise, despite the Sino–Japanese war, Japan was as yet unscreenable. One would like to think that this was out of shame for so many years of Yellow Peril propaganda but I suspect that the moviemakers lacked, as they say, a handle to depict a potential enemy. Less than three years later, the Japanese would be revealed on our screens as subhuman beasts, so unlike Uncle Harry's democracy-loving and Christ-fearing Chinese.

On the other hand, it was pretty hard for a Caucasian eye to tell beast from ally. In the Pacific, we soldiers were briefed on the difference between a life-size cardboard cut-out of a nude Chinese youth and one of a Japanese youth. The briefing officer noted such differences as the bandy-legs of the "Jap," so unlike the straight, smooth limbs of the "Chinaman." But the principal difference, he said, pointing his pointer, "Is that the Japs have a lot more pubic hair than the Chinks." Needless to say, mine was the only voice raised at the briefing. How, I asked, does one persuade a possible enemy to reveal this tell-tale difference?

On screen, one glimpsed Chinese warlords in *The Bitter Tea of General Yen* (1933), and *The Good Earth* showed us Okies, Confucian-style (1937). Germany was not yet demonized, while Hitler himself was treated with some nervousness. But the gentle majesty of England was everywhere depicted on every screen, while many of Hollywood's grandest film stars were English.

Particularly popular were the productions of an English-based Hungarian, Alexander Korda. He made his first great success with *Henry VIII*, whose baroque table manners, as demonstrated by Charles Laughton, set an awesome standard for the American child. Korda also befriended an out-of-office politician and journalist named Winston Churchill, who con-tributed several swatches of purple dialogue to at least one Korda film.

Fire Over England was released in 1937, rather early for this sort of gallant-little-England picture. I was enthralled. But then I had been a Tudor loyalist from my first encounter with that dynasty's propagandist, Shakespeare, and my essential role model never ceased to be Mickey Rooney, who, as Puck, proclaimed, "I'll put a girdle round about the earth in forty minutes." Well, I, too, had famously taken to the air for forty minutes, but I was undone by an inferior script. Had I not been sabotaged by my father's direction, Mickey and I might have changed places, and he would be a novelist today while I would be touring triumphantly in *Sugar Babies*. Life is unfair.

The young leads of *Fire Over England* were Laurence Olivier and Vivien Leigh in their first film together. Flora Robson was Elizabeth the First and Raymond Massey was the Hitlerlike king of Spain, who is about to launch a fleet against England. He is also Roman Catholic, and he means to overthrow the Protestant ascendancy established by Elizabeth's father, Henry VIII, better known to me as the father of Bobby or Billy Mauch in *The Prince and the Pauper*. Thanks to these films, one knew quite a lot about Tudor times. One also knew exactly what to think about *Fire Over England*, thanks to a series of title cards that start the film.

Apparently, King Philip rules by "force and fear," which is why he is played by the saturnine Raymond Massey, who also figures as the forcefully fearsome villain in *The Prisoner of Zenda*; then, two years later, he turns into Abraham Lincoln in *Abe Lincoln in Illinois*, another fiercely forceful sovereign, according to my Mississippi grandparents.

The first title card tells us: "In 1587, Spain, powerful in the old world, master in the new, its king, Philip, rules by force and fear." Hitler and Mussolini immediately spring to mind. The next title card offered hope. "But Spanish tyranny is challenged by the free men of a little island, England." It was safe now to start on the popcorn. A third card was somewhat confusing: "Everywhere English traders appear, English seamen threaten Spanish supremacy." We all knew that the famous British fleet was as impregnable as the Maginot line; and we knew from the newsreels that the British king liked to dress up as an admiral. But how could a bunch of traders turn into sailors, challenging Spain?

A fourth card appears out of left field: "A woman guides and inspires them, Elizabeth the Queen." Of course, there were not many of us in that audience who did not know that Elizabeth's father was Charles Laughton and that her mother, Merle Oberon, lost her head after wistfully stroking what she referred to as "such a tiny neck." We had also seen Elizabeth mistreat her cousin, Mary Queen of Scots, as played by Katharine Hepburn. The definitive Elizabeth, with Bette Davis, would not be screened until 1939, that *annum mirabilis* of the movies.

Even without this central text, I was among the few trained historians in the audience who wondered why I—that is, Bobby or Billy Mauch—wasn't king any longer? I now realize that British Intelligence had kept from us the poignant shortness of Edward VI's reign in order to build up his half-sister, Elizabeth, who successfully defied the dictator of the day, Philip, so like the Hitler of ours.

A few minutes into the movie, we are again told what to think by no less a personage than Lord Burleigh, an ancient courtier, who turns to a handy globe—there is always a globe in these scenes, seldom a map. He then proceeds to instruct the Vivien Leigh character in geography, something that she probably knew, but we out there in the movie houses of the great isolationist republic did not. "Here lies England," the old man croaked, "but half an island, not 300 miles long nor 200 miles broad. How small we are, how wretched and defenseless." He then contrasts the demi-island with all-powerful Spain. He is very glum.

Although a good actress, Flora Robson was not at her ease as a Renaissance sovereign. "I am England," she thunders; then, rather like Richard Nixon at his zenith, glances about furtively to make sure that no one has come to take her away. At the time, I couldn't help thinking how much more authoritative the Mauch twins and I would have been with such splendid dialogue, the work of Clemence Dane, a vigorous, somewhat megalomaniacal writer of the day. When asked if she would

44

The redoubtable Flora Robson as Gloriana—Our Queen! Despite the Revolution and 1812 and the bad blood over Britain's covert support of the Confederacy, British propaganda movies of the 1930s were making us all weirdly English.

like to adapt the Old and New Testaments of the Bible for the London stage, she said that she would be happy to do so, but she did wonder if the audience would feel cheated were she to omit Apocrypha.

Upon re-viewing and reflection, *Fire Over England* is unexpectedly bold in its condemnation of Catholicism, at least King Philip's brand. As someone remarks of the Spanish priests, "They herd souls as we do cattle." Worse, the script assures us that the struggle between little England and great Spain is actually a "war of ideas," something that might have given the original Elizabeth a good laugh, but caused our heads

45

to nod solemnly as we realized that our common Anglo past was again in peril and, as Lord Burleigh puts it, "We are servants in an old house who train the new servants." That was us all right, new servants of the old British Empire.

Four years later, the Korda team made pretty much the same film called, this time, *That Hamilton Woman*. Vivien Leigh played Lady Hamilton and Laurence Olivier played Lord Nelson. Our gallant little island is still not three hundred by two hundred miles in size, but it is menaced now not by a Spanish but by a French dictator while, in real life, the immediate menace in the newsreels was a German dictator. Again, the producer was Alexander Korda and, again, Winston Churchill

The inevitable geography lesson to make sure that the little island we would want to live and die for in the coming war was not imperial Japan but royal England.

It was a good thing for British intelligence that the two most beautiful as well as talented movie actors of the day were Vivien Leigh and Laurence Olivier. I have seen That Hamilton Woman *perhaps twenty times. Winston Churchill allegedly clocked one hundred viewings, but then he wrote a part of the film.*

helped out with the script, which was the work of one of the few true film auteurs, R. C. Sherriff, famous for the play *Journey's End* and the script of that near-perfect film, *Odd Man Out* (1947).

Churchill's mock-Macaulay speeches for Nelson jar badly with Sherriff's elegant dialogue, but patriot Olivier pulls it all together, as he warns everyone in sight not to do business with dictators, ever. There is also a map scene where "tiny little England" is carefully located for Emma Hamilton's benefit, not to mention ours. Even then, British Intelligence had no great faith in the American educational system.

Fire Over England

≈

From 1937 to 1941 we were treated to a hundred *Fire Over Englands*. Then the Japanese sank our fleet at Pearl Harbor with, according to our films, *absolutely no provocation at all* except that evil that resided—and still resides—in their collective, if not collectivist, souls. God knows what *their* films will be like now that they have bought Hollywood. I have a strange intuition —presentiment, call it what you will—*that they do not see us as we see us*. If I may say so with all due modesty, this is the sort of profound insight into the human heart that one gets from having viewed so much screened history.

I should note here—because I've not found any other place to do so—that a primary function of the narrative art is to produce empathy in those who may otherwise lack the ability to understand what it is that another person feels or thinks. America's famous disasters in the world at large and here at home are usually the result of an inability to get the point to others, not to mention ourselves. We do have our elective affinities but they are less the expression of a wise Jeffersonian electorate than the mean result of hanky-panky in that Cook County, Illinois, which has always presided over our affairs. In the interest of consumerism, solipsism is encouraged. Yet other people in other times have highly valued empathy, and grasped, if nothing else, its practical necessity.

Two thousand years ago, a standard exercise for a Roman schoolboy would be to write an essay as if he himself were some historical personage at a time of crisis. Marius among the ruins of Carthage was a favorite subject. This was not only a good way to teach history but it forced the schoolboy to place himself outside himself and inside the character of another person in another place and time. Today, not even professional actors like to do this. What they take to be sincerity requires that they always be themselves in the interest of what they call "truth." The results are often very boring, but then, as they are quick to remind us, so is most life.

Actors to one side, it is notable how little empathy is cultivated or valued in our society. I put this down to our traditional racism and obsessive sectarianism. Even so, one would think that we would be encouraged to project ourselves into the character of someone of a different race or class, if only to be able to control him. But no effort is made. A paper like the *Wall Street Journal* is able to give admirably precise analyses of corporate balance sheets, which are then interlarded with demented fictions where it is suggested that four fifths of a nation should go away.

Now I am sufficiently Hamiltonian to recognize that self-interest is not only central to each of us but a useful motor to the state; but an inability to recognize and accommodate that same interest in others is a receipt for chaos. Certainly, a nation untempered by Jefferson will be presided over by Hobbes. So —more empathy! Let that be your cry, as you plunge out into the night, and forsake John Harvard's holy puritan square for that squalid Scollay Square of all our ancient dreams and amusements, and for the sweaty reality, if not the kindness, of angels in disguise. We used to write like that in the forties. Tennessee Williams did to the end.

By the time the war came, we had been obliged to empathize with the British totally and with the French somewhat; with the Germans and the Japanese not at all. Of the pre-war films that deeply impressed me, many were biographical in nature and starred a splendid English actor called George Arliss. Among others, Mr. Arliss had impersonated Disraeli, Rothschild, Wellington, and, my favorite, Cardinal Richelieu. As I tended to read up on periods that appealed to me in the movies—my historian of choice was Rafael Sabatini, the Arthur

Schlesinger, Jr., of his day—the court of Louis XIII had become one of my favorite hang-outs, and I was always on the Cardinal's side.

The United States and its heroes, aside from westerns, were largely ignored. There were two films about Lincoln before he was president, none about Washington or Jefferson. Of the pre-war *American* films, the most notable was *The Grapes of Wrath*, a reasonably nonsentimental look at the Okies and their flight from the dust bowl. There was also Orson Welles' *Citizen Kane*. If Welles had been less prodigal with his great gifts, he might have screened a good deal more of our history for us. Welles was deeply political; he had worked with Roosevelt; he was a miracle of empathy, and he knew all the gradations of despair that the oyster experienced as it slid down his gullet. But the romantic genius aims not for perfection in his art but for poignant glamour in his ruin.

My first response to *Citizen Kane* was shock. There, on the screen, was William Randolph Hearst, my grandfather's ally and my father's enemy—our family tended to divide in such things. But thanks to Welles' empathy for the subject, I thought I understood Hearst, as I still do.

Then, in 1939, David O. Selznick gave us a significant part of our history in *Gone with the Wind*, just as we ourselves were about to become history, thanks to Franklin Roosevelt. Our generation, he told us—indeed, ordered us—had a rendezvous with destiny, all of it to be screened as it happened.

In June of 1939, at the age of thirteen, I set sail for Europe, with several boys and two masters from Washington's Saint Albans school. We were to spend a month "perfecting" our French near Versailles. Then on to Italy and England. War was about to break out, but we were intrepid. I could not wait to leap up, as it were, onto the screen where so much history had been revealed in fictions, not to mention in the history that we were now living through in newsreels and in propaganda movies.

Dover cliffs. Eiffel Tower. The battlefields of the First War, and the cemeteries where we saw poppies growing in glorious Technicolor, thanks to the mysterious yet ever-credited Natalie Kalmus. We saw the Maginot Line. These fortifications, the French assured the world, could never be breached by any mortal army. So Hitler sensibly went around them, to the consternation of the French general staff, for whom I had very little respect after their behavior in the Dreyfus case, where innocent Joseph Schildkraut was sent to Devil's Island. The next year, I was not entirely surprised when France fell despite the French soldier, the *poilu*, the finest fighting man on earth, according to Henry Luce and all the others who were busy screening the world for us.

On July 14, 1939, I stood on the steps of the Petit Palais and watched France display its military glory in a parade most notable for the North Africans, old comrades of mine from the Foreign Legion movie *Under Two Flags* (again division, doubleness). I was awed by the parade until I saw an open car containing a bald man in a business suit. I could spot a politician anywhere in any country. This one was the prime minister of France. He was called Daladier and he was known to the press as The Bull of Vaucluse. That July 14 he looked very nervous. Later, he proved to be more heifer than bull when he fell captive to the Germans.

Despite the heat of Rome in August, I was ecstatic. At last I was where I belonged. I haunted the Forum and the Palatine. In addition to all the Roman movies that I had seen, the first grown-up book that I ever read was a Victorian edition of *Stories from Livy*. I was steeped in Rome. I also lived in a city whose marble columns were a self-conscious duplicate of the old capital of the world. Of course Washington then lacked six of the seven hills and a contiguous world empire. Later, we got the empire but not the hills.

On a hot evening our group attended the outdoor opera in the Baths of Caracalla. *Turandot* was being staged. Next to us, under the stars, sat Mussolini. He wore a white uniform, and he looked almost as worried as Daladier. At the first intermission, he got up and left. As he passed within a yard of me, I got a powerful whiff of cologne, which struck me as degenerate. A moment later Mussolini was on the stage, taking a bow with the diva. The crowd shouted "Duce"; then he was gone.

At the end of August 1939 the border between Italy and France was shut. Luckily, we were aboard one of the last trains to get through. We hurried on to London, to Russell Square, Bloomsbury. On September first, when Germany invaded Poland, we stood outside Number 10 Downing Street and watched the prime minister, Neville Chamberlain, come out and get into his car, enroute to Parliament, where he would tell the world that war had come at last.

In those days, at fancy-dress parties, I used to dress up as Chamberlain, with a painted-on mustache and an umbrella in one hand and a paper, the Munich Agreement, in the other. Now there, in front of me, was the man that I had so often imitated. He was as small as I, and very thin, with a troublingly stringy neck enclosed by a wing collar that coyly revealed his gibbous Adam's apple. He gave a twitchy smile to the crowd in Downing Street, and they responded with a long collective sigh of a sort that I had not heard before, nor since.

When war was declared on September third, we were at Liverpool, aboard the British ship *Antonia*. As we entered the

Mickey Rooney as Puck in A Midsummer Night's Dream *(1935). He was my role model, though he must have been all of fourteen when I was only ten. Tennessee Williams once told me that he considered Rooney the best actor in the history of the movies.* A Midsummer Night's Dream *was Rooney's twenty-seventh film.*

Puck could be ten years old in this shot, but the hoarse voice is a giveaway—Rooney is already awash with testosterone and so imposter.

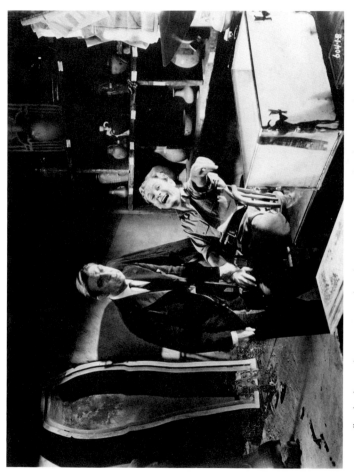

Bramwell Fletcher, playing an archaeologist, cannot stop laughing. He has just seen the mummy come to life, and gone mad. Twenty-two years later, in my first live play for television (Dark Possession), I asked him to recreate the laugh. "I have quite forgotten," he said, primly. I had not.

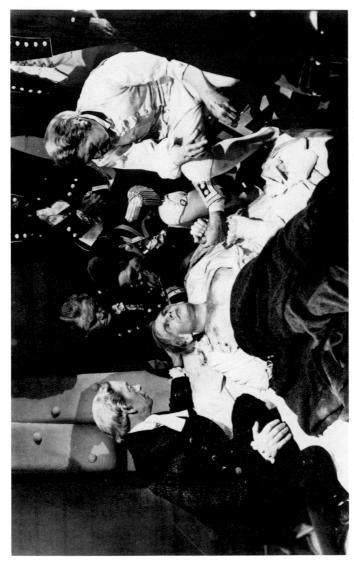

This is the height of heroism in That Hamilton Woman: *Nelson's last words to his loyal lieutenant, "Kiss me, Hardy." The world wept, and we all vowed that we could never let down so great a commander, or the island nation for which he gave his life. Nelson's actual (alleged) words to Hardy were suppressed: "Look after Lady Hamilton. The clap I gave her won't be good for business."*

Fire Over England, and will the young Olivier and Leigh be able to put out the flames for the sake of free men everywhere? Yes! They could and they did. The world was saved from the Spanish dictator Philip II, as it would be saved by Nelson from the French dictator Napoleon in the next century, as it would be saved by Churchill from the German Hitler in the twentieth century.

The ultimate cinematic irony proved to be the casting of Raymond Massey as the dark, brooding Catholic despot Philip of Spain; then three years later, Massey played, most memorably, Abe Lincoln in Illinois. Was a fan of Booth somehow involved with casting?

Irish Sea, we passed the *Antonia's* half-sunk sister ship, the *Athenia*, the first ship of the war to be torpedoed by a German submarine.

I remember a gray sky, and a gray smooth sea, and the longboats, containing passengers and ship's crew, making their way toward the dull green Irish shore. Adults aboard our ship wondered if we, too, would be sunk. As the "Boy Airman," I was fearless. For one thing, I had seen far more scary movies in my day than this one. I also could not imagine myself as a real-life victim since my *true* life was that of spectator at the drama of others, my empathy aroused only by *their* fictional sufferings, particularly that of the young Foreign Legionnaire who died so superbly in *Under Two Flags*, as the "Marseillaise" filled the sound track. He was real. I was not, except observing him.

In order to evade submarines, we zig-zagged across the North Atlantic. I was bored; and the ship's canteen ran out of chocolate. Upon arrival home, much was made of how my blond hair had turned dark: the result of war's horror some thought; others blamed puberty. At the barber shop in the basement of the Mayflower Hotel, I confessed to the barber that my hair had not been washed in three months. As I leaned over the wash bowl, black water cascaded in front of my eyes; and I was again as blond as Nelson Eddy.

That same year—1939—is considered the optimum year of Hollywood film-making. For an instant we were balanced on the radiant cusp between Depression's end and war's beginning. During my fourteenth year, I saw each of the now-classic films as it was released. It was a golden age, and I was not at all like Randall Jarrell's critic who, living through a golden age, kept complaining about how yellow everything was. It couldn't be gold enough for me.

Fire Over England

≈

Let me anticipate a question. During this time, did I ever see a *good* movie? The answer is, yes, I probably did, but how would I have known? For us, any movie was better than no movie. For us, the concept of a movie being aesthetically good or bad was as irrelevant as saying that a bit of history was good or bad. Obviously, one enjoys some moments of history, screened, written, or experienced, more than others but how is relative value to be determined of something which, like history, simply *is*? That was then.

As we got older, so did the movies and, in due course, it was discovered that the movies were an art form, which I would contest, and that since a work of art must be the conception of a single genius (like the cathedral at Chartres?), the French seized upon the idea of the director as *auteur*, with uncomfortable results. I would like to have heard my friend David Selznick on the subject. Like God, Selznick, and Selznick alone, had created the film of *Gone with the Wind* and only a master of the most trivial pursuits knew, even then, the name —or indeed, the names—of the disposable directors.

I was never conscious that movies were art in the way that some books or pictures on display at the new Mellon Gallery were art. Movies were real to us; and that was it. Some haunted the imagination; others did not. One that haunted me was the English-made *The Ghost Goes West*, directed by the French René Clair. I have now watched the picture for a second time. Incidentally, the video cassette has subtly altered the way that we perceive a movie. On the theater screen we notice what is bad; on the home monitor what is good. I have not thought through what this . . . democratization? means.

In eighteenth-century Scotland, Robert Donat runs away from a fight with another clan; he is killed, and his ghost is condemned to haunt the family castle until he has avenged the family honor. Two centuries later, the castle is sold and shipped, stone by stone, to America, where the ghost finally confronts a descendant of the rival clan, and in a fine scene of thunder and lightning, he brings him to his knees. Honor satisfied, he ascends to cloudy heaven. The ghost has a look-alike descendant who figures in the plot. Doubleness yet again.

I can't think why this story so appealed to me. Of course, there is the attractive conceit that personality survives death, even if one is only a ghost on a boring assignment. I suspect it was the confrontation with the rival clansman that excited me. I was brought up in the southern fashion, so wittily deplored by Henry Adams, where personal honor and clan loyalty are identical. This may explain why, over the last thirty years, I have done three screen versions of Billy the Kid, centered on the notion of loyalty to one's kind and a liking for things square.

In the fall of 1939, I was sent to a school for disturbed rich boys, although I was neither disturbed nor my father rich. But my mother was constantly on the alert for exotic schools, and the Los Alamos Ranch School in New Mexico took, as it were, the cake. Isolated on a spectacular mesa, seventy boys rode horses and led the strenuous life as laid down by Theodore Roosevelt, one of whose disciples had founded the school.

I suspect that my life-long aversion to Roosevelt began with the headmaster. He combined Rooseveltian strenuosity with an exuberant pederasty that would have excited the envy of Gilles de Rais. When I finally fingered the harasser to my family, one Patrick J. Hurley, a former secretary of war, was appealed to. He also had a son at the school. The boy was routed out of bed one night by his father and mercilessly grilled. Hurley then said that nothing that I had said was true because I was, in his curious phrase, "a greenhorn." Plainly, I had broken the code of *omertà* of the Old West. But little did they suspect that I was not the usual victim. I was already beginning to identify with Billy the Kid.

One year of the strenuous life was enough for me, and I was saved by a removal to Exeter. Meanwhile, the war came, and the government took over the school and the mesa in order to set up an atomic bomb laboratory. Today, in the museum of what is now a fair-sized city, I am told that my chaps are reverently displayed under glass. I shall never again see those chaps or that mesa. I *will* say that this small, if somewhat peculiar, school did produce two highly subversive writers. Myself and William S. Burroughs, whose homoerotic, not to mention sadomasochistic, fantasies I can trace directly to Theodore Roosevelt's vigorous disciple. I was left unaffected, my character already set as the Boy Airman in life and Edward VI on the screen. Poor Bill never saw enough movies.

I am now screening for you my own history because it intertwines with the actual history of our time. When I was at Exeter, George Bush was at Andover. He is a year my senior. More than once, he has confided to us that he has a problem with what he calls "the vision thing," not to mention the English language, which we at Exeter always thought somewhat neglected at Andover. But Bush's admission that he lacks vision of an ideological sort is hardly a surprise to any of us who were so educated and so brought up—in his case and mine by a senator in Washington.

For Americans of our place and time, ideology was incompatible with our DNA. Ideas, of course, were on offer, at least at Exeter. But visions were apt to lead to fantasy and worse, as Hitler was demonstrating. We were brought up in a real world of real politics, in a very real Washington. We knew the political game inside and out. Later, I chose out; Bush stayed inside. I make no judgment on either choice. But for Bush, brought up backstage, as it were, the playwright's vision is not always as easy to discern as the stage manager's homely business. It is also easier to take for granted the old saw that the show must go on than to grasp what the show is all about.

When one watched, as I did, Huey Long declaim—that is, rehearse—at the family table, and then hear him on the radio, and see him on screen in the newsreels, one realized to what an extent the whole thing is simply a calculated performance for the public. Losers at this game, like Bryan, had visions. Winners, like TR, had votes. Long after Roosevelt's presidency, his worshipful biographer, Hermann Hagedorn, confessed that he could never understand the great progressive's life-long adherence to the tariff, a major tenet of the worst elements of the Republican party. "Why?" asked Hagedorn, "*Why* did you support the tariff?" "Sheer expediency, dear boy," said the man of principle, "sheer expediency."

Those of us brought up backstage were as susceptible as anyone in the audience to the magic of a political performance, but we also knew, simultaneously, that the vision thing has nothing at all to do with the performing arts. It was not necessary to *be* the character, only to play him. The playwright was something else. He was the creator, the founder, and the United States, as far as we knew, had already been invented. Certainly, to date, no one has dared remodel the house since Lincoln so fundamentally rebuilt the whole thing—or rewrote the play, to continue the theatrical metaphor—out of *his* titanic rage at being a mere actor in a play by others.

I cannot think of a single Washington child who ever succumbed to an ideology of any sort beyond the usual conservative nostrums that we were all brought up with. For us, the only fault-line that ran through the republic's basement was

57

where the Jefferson–Hamilton tectonic plates meet and, in their near-perfect stasis, they have kept Lincoln's remodeled if still divided house from entirely caving in. Now, of course . . .

Recently, H. Stuart Hughes, a grandson of the awesome Chief Justice of my childhood, wrote of himself in a memoir called *Gentleman Rebel*. Older than I, he was attracted to socialism and to Debs but not to communism nor, indeed, to any formal ideology. He also did not spend as much time as I did hanging around the capitol. But he does describe listening to his famous grandfather, Charles Evans Hughes, give a commencement address. As he listened to the Jove-like old man, he was seized by "an inner discontent" which he sadly acknowledges was a Damascene vision to the glum effect that "what I was hearing was bullshit—there was no gainsaying it."

It was not until I got to Exeter in 1940 that I confronted head-on a lack of reverence for my grandfather. I felt not unlike the prince when captured by traitors. Proudly, I showed one of my teachers a copy of my grandfather's latest address, against going to war. The teacher sighed and said, "Well, he knows how to make the eagle scream." It was the first time that I had heard that phrase. Of course, I was in New *England*.

At my earlier Washington school, Saint Albans, political children were treated rather the way terminally ill children are treated. In a recent book one of the masters describes how the headmaster ordered him to steer clear of political discussions with the boys in class. The First Amendment burned before the teacher like a pillar of fire: Why? he asked. Because, said the headmaster, this year there are five major presidential candidates and each of the five has got one son here. Political children are fierce partisans.

Luckily for me, Exeter was far removed from the squalors and discontents of democracy. Tribunes of the people were not taken seriously in a place where the one question that any opinion elicited was, What do you mean? As opposed to, what do you feel you think? or think you feel? It was rough for a boy-demagogue.

Romantically, perhaps, I like to think that there was something more than actor's expediency to us populists. Certainly, we were the consistent protest-ants. We said no to the money while those with the money had said no to the people. Since tribunes of the people were as much for sale in those days as now, my grandfather could easily have sold out, as could the stupid but noble William Jennings Bryan; but neither did. In fact, Bryan resigned as secretary of state rather than support Wilson's war policy. Senator Gore died poor.

When the Chamber of Commerce of Oklahoma City ordered my grandfather to vote for war in 1917, he sent the Chamber a telegram, asking them how many of their members were of draft age. They defeated him for re-election in 1920. This may be bullshit, in a way, but there is a populist principle behind it, not to mention an abiding dislike and mistrust of the ownership of the country as reflected not only in the sameness of the two parties but in what is now called the media.

Where I part company with my contemporary from Kennebunkport, Texas, is that he has no known political principles or even opinions other than how to master the stage-business necessary for him to take the temporary lead in a play he knows by heart but has not, perhaps, taken to heart.

On the other hand, I come from the Jefferson side of the fault, and I shared the family's belief that as government must be based on something, it should be based upon the people at large; and that foreign adventures were not only bad for character but, often as not, as we now know, even worse for business.

But I veer into demagoguery, the outward sign of the populist's inner grace. I have deployed more autobiography than even I can bear. Nabokov's *Speak, Memory* should now be superseded by *Shut Up, Memory*, as one grows garrulous. But then, when Lady Blessington interrupted Lord Byron's denunciation of Thomas Moore on the ground that Moore was his friend, Byron said, "Madam, I cannot stop. The fit is upon me."

The teacher at Exeter who opened my eyes to the "vision thing" was the one who so disdained Senator Gore's oratorical style. Thomas Riggs taught English; his father had been . . . no, you will never guess . . . governor of Alaska, the dull quotidianal Alaska whose capital is not Duluth and whose statehood was then no more than an icy dream. Riggs and I, for different reasons, were as one when it came to isolation versus intervention. Riggs was radical in politics and radical in literature, at least by Exeter's highly conservative standards.

Riggs was a jug-eared, bald young man of great charm. When obliged to take over morning chapel, he would pull his clothes on over pink and white striped pajamas, plainly visible at wrist and ankle, and read the lesson and announcements in a voice like W. C. Fields. He gave his fans great joy, and he gave Lewis Bliss Perry, the principal, a headache.

A few years earlier, at Princeton, Riggs had organized a group of antiwar radicals. They called themselves the VFW— the Veterans of Future Wars. They insisted that they be paid their bonuses *before* they were wounded or killed in the approaching war to put out that fire over England. I led the America First group at Exeter, with Riggs back of me. But the Bundles for Britain group was far stronger and, led by my nemesis, one T. W. Lamont, Jr., grandson of J. P. Morgan's partner, they won.

On the day after Pearl Harbor, we gathered in a common room to listen to Roosevelt's declaration of war. At the end, Lamont gave me a triumphant sneer. He was my first William

Buckley. But his subsequent death at sea in a submarine at least convinced me of his seriousness. But we were all serious then, at least those who were politically minded, and we lived in what we took to be a serious country where each, in due course, would play as great a role as he could.

I would be curious to know to what extent Bush took part in the debate between isolation and intervention. I do find in his disjointed speeches and mumbled asides many echoes of those films that so affected all of us, not to mention the endless newsreels of Roosevelt and Churchill, two powerful demagogues for whom the actual fate of nations must have been as unreal as a play is to a star when he is not himself at centerstage.

December 7, 1941, the debate over war and peace, empire and republic, came to a temporary end. In 1917 Wilson had predicted that those oligarchs of capital whom he had tried to tame in his first administration would now, under the excuse of wartime emergency, re-establish a more perfect boardroom state, which they did; and it lasted until the Depression.

After 1941 the same thing happened again. The famous dollar-a-year businessmen came to town to put the war on a business-like footing. Dr. New Deal, as FDR airily explained, had given way to Dr. Win-the-War. So we won the war and lost the deal. The businessmen found that they had so enjoyed running the United States that they set up that National Security State in which we still live, and where two thirds of the federal revenues must go for war until Depression or defeat— or whatever—comes again and puts a stop to a half-century of waste and corruption.

In June of 1943 I graduated from Exeter and a month later, at seventeen, I enlisted in the Army of the United States, as a private. Unlike the soldiers of the First War, at least as reported by poets and novelists, we were not enthusiasts. To the extent that we knew anything about Hitler's crimes, they were remote from us. Even that fire over tiny little England had not really made us interventionists. What did the trick was the astonishing nerve of a yellow race, our inferior in every way save, perhaps, pubic hair, which had had the nerve to blow up the American fleet at Pearl Harbor, *without warning*. It is the lack of warning that is truly intolerable, as Saddam Hussein will testify.

Lately, in our military adventures, we are careful to proclaim that we are never against the people of a country, only against their evil leaders. But in that war we reveled in the thought of absolute genocide. The Japanese were an evil race and should be destroyed. They were incessantly screened for us as truly monstrous, not a hard thing to do as the yellow peril is a permanent part of the American psyche and needs little stimulus to burst its cage, particularly today when the white race, to which most Americans pledge proud allegiance, comprises less than a fifth of the world's population.

So here we are, a declining world power, governed by a minority race with many well-deserved enemies. We use fifty percent of the world's energy, and so on and so forth. Now, if you were George Bush, shaped by the same movies that shaped us all in the thirties, what would you do next, having played, in a small way, Errol Flynn in the sands of Mesopotamia? What will a politician so bred do next in order to show the audience that he is as great as Raymond Massey or Henry Fonda or, as those two superstars of real-life history, Roosevelt and Churchill?

Those who lived through, as well as watched, the screened history of this century know that the field of glory is pretty well harvested, "and the crop is already appropriated. But new reapers will arise, and they too will seek a field. It is to deny what the history of the world tells us is true to suppose that men of ambition and talents will not continue to spring up amongst us. And when they do, they will as naturally seek the gratification of their ruling passions as others have done before them." You will, of course, recognize the words of the young Abraham Lincoln, warning us against himself, which brings us, next, to *Lincoln*. And to . . . *George Bush?*★

★When George Bush was elected president in 1988, I predicted on "Larry King Live" that he would be another Herbert Hoover and serve only one term. You, the reader, will know if I was right.

Henry Fonda in the last frame of The Young Mr. Lincoln. *A haunting silhouette: he is about to turn left at the top of a hill, and into a terrible storm, taking us all with him—our ancestors, that is,*

Lincoln

≈

I still have a silver cup that I won as first prize for sand modeling at Bailey's Beach, Newport, Rhode Island. It was the summer of 1936 and we were living in the Van Alen house, Ma Folie, better known as Ma's Folly, while my stepfather, with characteristic patience, waited for his mother to die so that he could move into Hammersmith Farm where the old lady still presided over two liveried footmen as well as a conservatory that produced out-of-season grapes, more beautiful than a Vermeer painting, and about as tasteless. In those days, I was not only the Boy Airman of the newsreels but a Renaissance talent, rather like Newport-born Clarence King, so admired by Henry Adams. I drew, I sculpted, I wrote, I read nearly a book a day, and I saw the movies, and understood from them the world. As you might guess, I was a royal pain in the ass, a role that I still do my best to fulfill even now, in the springtime of my senescence.

Small talents often come in a cluster, and there are numerous cases of the writer who can draw and the painter who can write and the composer who can do logarithms. In youth, I was the repository of a myriad of mediocre talents, and that high summer at Newport I was in my Gutzon Borglum phase. When there was a contest for the best creation of a figure in sand, quite a job on a beach almost entirely covered with seaweed and gelatinous rotting Portuguese men-of-war, I won the prize with a larger-than-life head of Abraham Lincoln.

For someone in my situation, a condition of aging is that one is besieged by biographers. They are almost as numerous and insistent as fundraisers from the Alumni Association of the Philips Exeter Academy who, as shadows lengthen, circle one's head like buzzards, when not flying in formation in order to spell out against the sky the chilling phrase: Estate Planning.

Let me note that the buzzard-biographers are not all mine. They are writing about friends and acquaintances, too. I seldom respond to any of them, as I don't much care for that memory road, which diverged for me, so long ago, in a yellow wood. For me the yellow *brick* road still lies ahead, and every buzzard is a bluebird, and if that is not a rainbow that I see before me then I do have glaucoma.

But so much nudging, as it were, has made me think, occasionally, about myself as opposed to others. Earlier, I spoke of empathy. Thanks in part to movies, my own was enlarged at the expense of myself. That is why, as a writer, I have seldom been my own subject.

Now, in response to the questioning of scholars, I have succumbed—am succumbing, anyway—to the American writer's disease, the celebration if not of self, of the facts of one's own sacred story. Whitman was the first to *triumph* in the field; he turned the Cosmos into himself. But few writers are so titanic. I think that I have always been able to imagine what it is like to be someone else, but now I begin to wonder what it is like to be me, a figure that keeps cropping up in the lives of others, usually wearing an impenetrable disguise.

I have started to go through old papers and notebooks. Along with the tarnished first prize for sand modeling—a beautiful if somewhat too neat metaphor for the arts at this end of the century—I have found a notebook in which I have drawn, from a photograph, the face of Abraham Lincoln. Beneath it, I wrote, in a reverent if slovenly hand, "Now he belongs to the ages." What was this all about, Lincoln and I?

In our time, the screening of Lincoln has been every bit as inadequate as the prosing of Lincoln. There was the actor Raymond Massey as Lincoln, at home in Illinois, quarreling with his wife; and there was the very young Henry Fonda as Lincoln, practicing law and burying, quite early in the film, Ann Rutledge, a minor blessing; and that was pretty much that. Impersonations by Walter Huston and John Carradine were not truly iconesque. Lincoln was a god-like presence in other films such as *The Littlest Rebel*, starring Shirley Temple, a child actress who, at the age of six, sued Graham Greene for suggesting that she was a sexual provocateur. She won her case and became American ambassador to Czechoslovakia. I suppose it could have been worse. Certainly, to the day of his death, Greene lived in terror of Shirley Temple's wrath.

One wonders, not so idly, what sort of a country we might have had if, instead of being bombarded by the screened versions of Nelson and Napoleon and Queen Elizabeth, we had been given films about Jefferson and Hamilton and the Lincoln presidency. Certainly, the *agon* between Jefferson and Hamilton that still continues after two centuries is of enduring fascination to anyone who finds our republic at all interesting. For a number of reasons that I shall try to address, I doubt if we shall now ever get the mythical works that we need, and by myth I do not mean falsified or romanticized history so much as those tribal narratives that define the prospect, much as the western light gave a certain beauty to silent films where the director dared not photograph anyone at noon because so full fierce a light distorts features.

If Lincoln was so inadequately screened, then why did Lincoln so preoccupy me? There was the temple, of course, at the heart of the city. Once I got interested in Rome and Greece, I used to haunt that part of Washington, imagining myself in ancient Rome. Now when I visit what has become a Disneyland Federal Theme Park, I imagine myself in ancient America, so long ago does our republic seem to me. I also remember when they were building the nearby memorial to Jefferson. I liked it until they set up that crude statue; then I took against the enterprise, much as I've always taken against Jefferson the man, whom I find disagreeable in his sanctimonious hypocrisy, as opposed to Jefferson the god, who gave us the idea that it was legitimate to pursue happiness in a present which, Jefferson said, belonged to the living. This was a novel concept in a sectarian society such as ours where we are expected to endure meekly our brief transit through a vale of tears en route to an eternity of bliss.

Now is now, was Jefferson's view, and now is all there is for us—ever—now. I do not know to what extent Jefferson consciously influenced my beloved Alexander Herzen, but Herzen's famous rhetorical question, from the other shore, in every sense, is the essential Jefferson: "Do you truly wish to condemn the human beings alive today to the sad role of caryatids supporting a floor for others some day to dance on . . . ?" I would like to have seen *that* Jefferson screened. Hamilton, as well. But so far the screen is dark, and we have no electronic Virgil, much less Homer. We don't even have a Parson Weems. We have only the Rich and Famous who have lifestyles, rather than lives.

Of the members of my family, I was closest to my grandfather because I had to read to him when my grandmother periodically wore out. She read beautifully, in a low melodious southern voice; she also read without the slightest attention to the *matter* of what she was reading. We used to gather round whenever she read of some bloody murder, her mind far away, as the awful details fell gently from her lips, like gardening hints. Occasionally, she would rebel and if no secretary was at hand, I would be sent for. I would read. Then the old man would talk, about everything.

I can't remember much that Senator Gore had to say about Lincoln. He did talk about his friend, Lincoln's son, Robert, who had told him that he and his father had not got on well. Then a constituent from Oklahoma came to Washington: She was writing a book about President Lincoln. Could Senator Gore arrange a meeting with Robert Lincoln? Always dutiful when it came to the constituency, my grandfather gave the woman and Robert Lincoln lunch. "Mr. Lincoln, I have absolute proof," she announced over the Senate's renowned bean soup, "that your mother was the illegitimate daughter of John C. Calhoun." That was the last my grandfather ever saw of Robert Lincoln.

Although T. P. Gore was a Mississippi populist who had kept the faith, he was by no means provincial in his taste. He was also not superstitious. When his father became a Campbellite, a form of relatively intellectual fundamentalism, Gore not only refused to follow his father into the Campbellite church but declared himself an atheist, and so remained to the end of his days. Needless to say, he did not share his secret with the Oklahoma constituents. I took after him; and I, too, have kept the nonfaith.

I was shocked to find that my grandfather had no high opinion of Lincoln's prose. When I recited the Gettysburg Address for him, he took me *back* of the music to the sense of the speech, which appalled him. Lincoln was celebrating the men that he had caused to die in a war of his own making, to preserve a union of states that did not choose, a number of them, to be united. As for government of, by, and for the people, that was perfect nonsense and Lincoln knew that it was.

Lincoln
≈

When I asked him what politician's style he did admire, he said, unexpectedly, John Bright. Bright was a political master of the House of Commons in the year of my grandfather's birth, 1870. A true liberal in the old American sense, Bright stood with the working classes in the battle for Reform. Bright's phrase "a free breakfast table" became our "no free lunch." Bright hated war as much as did Gore—and I—and Bright's speech against the war in the Crimea is almost as memorable as that of Pericles' belated report to the Athenians. My grandfather knew much of it by heart: "The angel of death has been abroad throughout the land; you may almost hear the beating of his wings." One wonders what effect this 1855 speech had on Lincoln, who certainly knew it, though he was dead by the time John Bright had formulated that unquestionable truth: "Force is not a remedy."

From the screened Lincoln of my childhood I learned of Dr. Mudd, who had lived not too far from where I lived at Merrywood. Mudd tended the broken ankle of John Wilkes Booth the night that he shot Lincoln: and was duly punished for his good deed. Even though there was so little of Lincoln screened, I have always had the sense that I had been present at the Cooper Union speech, delivered on his way to Exeter to see his son or, as the son put it, on his way to the White House by pretending to visit his son while presenting himself to New England's voters. I can also visualize the First and Second Inaugural Addresses but that is thanks to Mathew Brady; and then, over and over again, I see the cemetery at Gettysburg, I see Ford's Theater, and the gun, and the slow train west.

I did read Carl Sandburg's six-volume scrapbook about Lincoln, but these books made less impression on me than the face of Raymond Massey on the screen, or that of Henry Fonda, pleading with a mob not to lynch someone without due process. I am not a devotee of the director John Ford, but he and his cameraman achieved a moment at the picture's end which still demonstrates that the right picture can be equal, almost, to the right word.

Fonda has won a legal case. He is thanked by the young couple that he has saved. They go. A yokel remains. A storm threatens. "Ain't you going back, Abe?" Fonda shakes his head. "I think I might go on a piece," he says. "Maybe to the top of that hill." He is wearing a frock coat, and the stove-pipe hat with which the national icon is associated.

As Fonda climbs the hill, the camera is behind him. At the top of the hill, there is a reverse angle shot, with the camera below him. The medium-sized actor suddenly appears tall, elongated, a sort of engraving upon the cloudy sky. There is lightning now, and thunder. The figure pauses, as if considering whether or not to take shelter. Then he turns to the left at the top of the hill, and walks straight into the storm; and it is no longer a shadowed light that we see upon the screen but Lincoln himself, reduced to an essence. The year of that film's release was the great year—for movies—1939.

By 1944 I was a nineteen-year-old Warrant Officer in the Army of the United States with a commission as first mate aboard an army freight supply ship. Why was the Boy Airman of yesteryear not an army flyer? Acute myopia had grounded me—or, rather, set me afloat. On a bright autumn day we boarded a troop ship in Seattle. An army band played "The Trolley Song," from the film *Meet Me in St. Louis*, a song that even then I associated with Walt Whitman. That day, on the gangplank, I was no longer the fearless Boy Airman of 1936 who had so blithely endured the submarine-infested North Atlantic. I was a writer, able to imagine his poignant death at sea: or, indeed, anywhere else.

We had not been told where our ship was headed. The

fact that we had been issued winter gear suggested the South Pacific. But I knew, somehow, that Alaska would be my destination. Alaska, and beyond. To the Aleutian Islands, that necklace of jasper and moonstone set in the black icy Bering Sea.

I was assigned to Army Freight Supply Ship 35. We operated out of Chernowski Bay on the island of Umnak; once a week we sailed with passengers and supplies to Dutch Harbor and back. At Dutch Harbor I saw a movie a night in a large wooden warehouse. As Walt Whitman remarked, the true story of a war is never told by anyone who was there. I shall merely note, in passing, that in that womanless society, with only intelligent ravens for company, the vision of the founder of the Los Alamos Ranch School was made incarnate. But I leave that sort of thing to William S. Burroughs. Who amongst us would want to hear of polymorphic perverse sex beside the Bering Sea, when we might closely analyze Lincoln's fiat monetary system as devised by Salmon Portland Chase?

The death of Franklin Roosevelt was hugely screened while I was in the Army hospital at Anchorage, recovering from overexposure—to the elements, in this case, not the media. First, we heard it on radio; then from the newspapers; then it was confirmed upon the screen. It seemed impossible that this larger-than-life King Kong of a newsreel politician was gone. I was delighted, of course. He had got us into the war; he had established a dictatorship; he had defeated my grandfather in the election of 1936. He was also the only president that I could remember, and I was bored to death with him. As the years passed, I came to admire Roosevelt's New Deal, if only for the wonderfully messy improvisatory nature of the thing. There was no plan. There was no new deal, or any deal at all except that of a very wily, bold card-player who, once he'd lost a hand, would say, Let's deal again.

At the wheel, Warrant Officer (Junior Grade) Eugene Luther Gore Vidal (b. 1925), First Mate of the Army Freight Supply Ship 35. We operated out of Chernowski Bay on the island of Umnak in the Aleutians (winter 1944–45). Our usual run was to Dutch Harbor and back with supplies and passengers. I was a dangerously poor navigator, but at least my luck was better than Lord Jim's. Out of this experience came a first novel, Williwaw (1946).

Lincoln
≈

After the war I moved back to the Hudson Valley where I had been born, and I became a friend of the Widow Roosevelt. I also came to know a good bit about the making of that astonishing drama, the Roosevelt saga, as viewed from backstage. For instance, the Eleanor screened in the Rose Garden as Franklin is buried is not what it looks to be, a study in wifely grief, but rather it is the rage of Medea. She had discovered that an old mistress had been with him at the moment of death. It was my impression that Eleanor admired the president but disliked the husband. But whatever their personal feelings as actors, they were forever co-starred in the conscious and unconscious minds of every American then alive, and they themselves were quite aware of their own proto-fictiveness.

In Eleanor's coolly unsentimental memoir, she describes the train ride north from Georgia, with the President's body aboard, and how the long line of mourners beside the track reminded her of Lincoln's funeral train. Thus, Lincoln continued to haunt us all, including another presidential widow who would insist on recreating as much as possible Lincoln's funeral, not an easy thing to do without lilac or Lincoln.

Of the scene in the Rose Garden, Eleanor told me that they had not yet read the President's will. Later, she was startled to read that he wanted to be buried in a coffin with one side open. Since she hadn't known this at the time, he lies to this day in a standard coffin. Why, she wanted to know, the open side? I knew the answer. Indeed I *know* I know the answer to a question that puzzled the family: The President wanted to get back into circulation as quickly as possible, and what better way than for his molecules to be incorporated immediately into his own rose garden—or Roose-velt? She thought that I might be right. She herself was not one to dwell on death or the afterlife. She was deeply annoyed when the Dutch Queen Wilhelmina, on a visit to Hyde Park, spent much of her time

Here I am amid Alaskan, if not "Alaskan," snow. I ended up in an Army hospital, first at Fort Richardson, Anchorage, then at Birmingham General, Van Nuys, California: rheumatoid arthritis due to exposure.

talking to the dead through a medium. "Since one will be dead for so very long oneself," said Eleanor, "I cannot see why one should waste one's time talking to them now."

In due course, in her own lifetime, Eleanor saw herself memorably screened. This was 1960, the year that I ran for Congress. I had come to Hyde Park to discuss political strategy with Eleanor. Suddenly, there was the actress Greer Garson standing before us, dressed in turn-of-the-century clothes and wearing enormous false teeth in imitation of Eleanor's own renowned choppers.

Do I look all right? the actress wanted to know. Oh, yes, yes! Mrs. Roosevelt squeaked her approval. Such a nice dress, too, so much nicer than any I ever wore. But all the time that Eleanor was speaking, she was staring with fascinated horror at the actress's mouth, crowded with huge teeth. Finally, Miss Garson retired. Eleanor was reflective. Must movies be *quite* so realistic? she asked. Surely, my teeth are not so very—*large?* I told her that Miss Garson's make-up was simply a caricature of the original who was, in life and in her own way, beautiful.

That same year I screened my grandparents for the television audience in a play called *The Indestructible Mr. Gore.* The senator was dead by then, but my grandmother lived. The play was about their courtship, during which he—a blind man— was accused of making a blind girl pregnant. Thanks to this scandal, he lost an election for Congress but won my grandmother. William Shatner was the screened T. P. Gore, and I played myself, the grandson-narrator from the future. The play was popular. But then, as storage space has always been at a premium with NBC, they destroyed the tape. Even so, I was pleased to have screened with great accuracy one small bit of American history. Then the senator's brother told me, with bitter joy, that T. P. Gore had indeed knocked up the blind

Between 1954 and 1960 I wrote a number of plays for television. These one-hour plays were performed live, and most of the country watched them. Then live drama was eliminated altogether in favor of quiz shows. My last play was The Indestructible Mr. Gore, *with William Shatner as my twenty-five-year-old grand-father-to-be and Inger Stevens as his wife-to-be. I acted as narrator, from the future, wandering in and out of scenes. The play went on air December 13, 1959. Everyone seemed to enjoy it, including my dying grandmother. As usual, no kinescope has survived. We wrote, literally, on air.*

girl and that their mother had adopted the resulting child. History is not easy, whether screened or prosed. Pontius Pilate's question should be Cleo's motto.

Throughout my youth I seldom mentioned my family in school or in the army or among the literary people that I met. After my third novel, *The City and the Pillar*, it was thought that I was a farm boy from Virginia who had made good as a professional tennis player and part-time prostitute. I quite liked having people believe this. Certainly my backhand was much feared. The reason for pretending to so much ordinariness in my background had much to do with the kind of "truthful" realism so much admired then.

By and large, serious fiction was the work of victims who portrayed victims for an audience of victims who, it was oddly assumed, would want to see their lives realistically portrayed. No one serious would dream of writing about our rulers—or victimizers—because what truly serious writer would have known—or wanted to have known—them? For better or worse, this has been pretty much the main line of the Anglo-American novel from the artful George Eliot down to the not-so-artful present.

For me to use the world that I came from would mean that what I wrote would *look* to be very like the fantasy or day-dream narratives of best-sellerdom. In time, I would take that risk, but, unluckily for me, to be a true success in this line, the author must know as little about his subject as the reader. Writer and reader are then as one in imagining together a Marilyn Monroe, say, that never was. The only reality required by popular fiction is that the description of luxury goods with brand-names be precisely rendered.

I turned from the world I knew to invented worlds. I made Duluth capital of Alaska. I also began to relive past times, before my birth, before, indeed, that of our republic, which has never ceased for very long to be my subject.

I suppose it was inevitable that someone who had seen so many movies would eventually make them. As I needed money, I began to write plays for live television. This collective art form flourished from 1950 to 1960. As an hour-length play was acted, it would be photographed by three cameras. This meant that one wrote for the cameras as much as for the actors. I enjoyed myself very much. For one thing, the whole country watched those plays. Unfortunately, the programs were controlled by advertising agencies, and there was heavy censorship. Even so, I managed to write a play about a man who kills a figure like Senator Joe McCarthy out of a disinterested sense of justice.

It was during my time in television that I was confronted, at first hand, not only with the infamous blacklist but with the fierce way that censorship was—and is—exercised in our free country, a self-styled light to the world in general and to Asia in particular that Korean season. At the time, we believed that the brutal censorship was simply the result of a red-baiting maverick senator from Wisconsin. Actually, as we now know, the weather was being generated from the newly established National Security State, presided over by Harry S Truman, who had introduced the Federal Employee Loyalty Program in 1947. Six and a half million Americans were obliged to submit to this humiliating oath. We were rapidly losing the old republic; but that sort of bad news spreads slowly.

To say that I was politicized by all of this would be wrong. In a sense, you cannot politicize the political. I knew how politics worked. I never became a communist or even a socialist—except in my sympathies—because I knew that subscribing to any ideology would be pointless in a country so organized as ours. For instance, there has never been—and never can be—a labor party in the United States, because organized labor has been both harassed and demonized by government and media. Unless one really wanted to overthrow the state, communism was for me an exercise in group therapy at best, and a political orgone box at worst.

I know exactly how Bush of Mesopotamia sees the world because I see it as he does, but Bush has never questioned any of it as he scrambled up the conventional ladder, while I pushed the ladder away and drifted off into the vision thing.

The world that George Bush and I were shaped by was one where there were many elections but few if any politics. Occasional disagreements over matters of war and peace were determined not by the electorate but by the money-power and those who ritually served it and, as ritually, I sometimes sadly think, opposed it.

For our generation, the overthrow of the Japanese in the Pacific and the Germans in Europe was inevitable. Next, inevitably, we would take on an authoritarian (or was it totalitarian) ideology—communism—and the satanic empire that it had spawned where once was Holy Russia. All of this has been so intensely screened over the last half-century that any suggestion that we have never known what we were doing is sure to be ridiculed. Meanwhile, our genius for the metamorphosis of mere fact has achieved perfection.

The war in the Persian Gulf was one thing on CNN, and quite another in the European press. What it was in actual fact we may never know. All we do know is that what our government wanted to screen was screened and all else was off-camera and so nonexistent. Could we have lost this war? We may never know, one way or the other.

The first time that the screening of history became truly fabulous was after we lost our long and pointless war in Vietnam. This defeat, screened daily on television, was then meta-morphosed into a total victory in the *Rambo* movies, films which not only convinced everyone that we had, thanks to Mr. Stallone, won that war but which made almost as much money at the world box office as we had wasted on the war itself.

In the end, he who screens the history makes the history. If I were a would-be foreign conqueror of the United States, my cry to my hordes would be: Hollywood Delenda Est. If I could not destroy Hollywood, I would buy it, as the *Tora! Tora! Tora!* folks are now doing. From Columbia Pictures to mighty MCA-Universal, the Japanese are in control, and as they will shape our dreams in the end, I doubt very much if they will screen Lincoln for us or any of our history. Currently, they are influencing a Universal film about a crude American baseball player who joins a Japanese team, where he is taught good manners and docility by an older and subtler race.

Screen-writing has been my second career for close to forty years. By and large, my generation of writers did not become schoolteachers; if we needed money, we took a job at Columbia—the studio, *not* the university. What I began out of financial need I have persisted in out of fascination. In a sense, the movies lost their singular power when television was invented. The screen was literally shrunk, and what had once been a rare exciting vast spectacle screened in the dark of an exotic palace became a small, prosaic moving picture made up of a thousand lights behind the glass of a household appliance. Thus history is daily screened for us by network and cable news programs.

I suspect that even our pre-Japanese view of the world was more controlled and limited than that of Oblomov and his coffeehouse friends. Also, where he could always tell when government censors had been at work on the text of a news-paper, we have no idea at all what happened or did not happen in, say, the Persian Gulf. We also have no idea, as I write, which of our grateful allies has paid us compensation for that war—compensation is, of course, a euphemism for extortion.

As for the screening of our past, it has rarely been done. When it *is* attempted, the aim of the exercise is to teach simple patriotism to a people become so heterogeneous that many of them have little or nothing in common with one another, including, often, the English language. Plainly, it is not easy to inculcate patriotism when there is no agreed-on patria.

From the beginning of my not-so-happy career as a dramatist, I was drawn to politics and to religion, the only two subjects that Bernard Shaw thought worth our attention and, of course, the two subjects absolutely forbidden us not only in the popular arts but in the public schools as well. Public schools do not give us our history; instead, they try, nobly but futilely, to indoctrinate their charges in good citizenship. As each minority gains economic power, it is discussed in admiring terms. This is very good civics, but it is hardly history or even politics, since a text with no context is meaningless. Periodically, effort is made to present our founders as gods; these efforts fail.

Lately, ordinary families have taken to tracing their roots as far back into history as they can go; and they also hold annual get-togethers to discuss their findings. Recently, I attended Gore Day in Mississippi, where I gazed with some anguish upon two hundred variations of my own nose. It is humbling to realize that one's nose—persona, too—is just a bit of genetic encodement temporarily housed in a somewhat haywire molecular envelope, soon to be dispersed, with relief, if I may strike the plangent personal note.

My seventh or so cousin, Albert Gore, the future president, stayed away on my account. But then I disapprove of his fearsome wife, "Tipper," the scourge of the First Amendment. Last year there was a reunion of my grandmother's family, the Kays, which neither I nor my fifth cousin Jimmy Carter attended. So what the tribes cannot get in the schools, they now seek through genealogy and through the web of kinship. There is something not only touching but primal in this coming-together of blood kin. But, touching or not, this Homeric reversion to tribal life is no way to inspire a country, or, perhaps, the better verb would be to "invent" a country.

When I wrote for television I was able, every now and then, to comment on power as exercised in the great republic. Then I moved to Hollywood, where I wrote movies for MGM. As one always had more freedom in writing of the past than of the present—that is, if the past was not American—I took to writing such gorgeous junk as *Ben Hur*. Here I was at least able to present the serious Tiberius of Tacitus rather than the scurrilous caricature of Suetonius. My Tiberius resembled a hard-working but totally ineffectual chief executive of a lousy company like Chrysler.

In due course, I wrote plays that were staged on Broadway. One of them was called *The Best Man*, about a contest for the presidency between a man with a virtuous public life and a messy private life, and a man with a vicious public life and a private life beyond reproach. A former president acts as chorus and referee. The play was a success. The studios began to bid for the screen rights. At last I would be able to make my own movie. What follows is a paradigm of how rigidly our history and our politics are screened for us and how seldom anyone is allowed to reveal anything as it is.

United Artists bought the film rights. I would be a sort of producer as well as the writer of the screenplay. Then it was announced that the great Frank Capra would produce and direct. As I have noted, I never liked his political films. Even at twelve, I knew too much about politics to be taken in by his corny Mr. Smith coming to my town. Capra's movies usually pitted the good guy, Jimmy Stewart, to be admired because he has been elected to the Senate without any understanding of politics, against the bad guys who want to build a dam when what the folks really need is a new river, or the other way around.

What was I to do with Mr. Capra? My play was unusual; it was not only political but it was accurate, though Jack Kennedy did say to me, "When you're running for president, you don't have all that time to sit around and discuss the meaning of it all." Plainly, the vision thing is a hang-up of writers.

Frank Capra was an engaging and lively Sicilian-American. But age had made Capra, if possible, more sentimental than he had been in his youth. I had already lost two films based on my work, *The Left-Handed Gun* and *Visit to a Small Planet*. In each case, the wrong director had made the wrong film. I was not about to lose a third one. But how to get rid of Capra? The French *auteur* virus had already infected Hollywood, and dozens of brothers-in-law of producers who had spent years locked up on sound stages with actors no one wanted to talk to were now being treated as if they were singular creators, so many Leonardos, sprung, as it were, from the good earth of the San Fernando Valley. Of these auteurs, Capra was an acclaimed master, at least by *Cahiers du Cinema*.

Capra and I discussed the script a number of times. The realism of the piece did not impress him because, for him, politics was not what it is but what he himself had screened. As William Wyler studied not Roman history but other Roman movies in preparation for *Ben Hur*, so Capra tried to conform my, to him, disagreeable realism with the screened America that he was used to; that he had, in fact, helped invent. Once again the story was to be about the good guy who speaks for all The Little People.

Suddenly, Capra was inspired. "Let's open this up," he

said, small bright eyes like black olives. "At the convention, on the first day, our good guy—we'll get Stewart or maybe Fonda—he goes out into the crowd, where all these little people are the—you know, delegates . . ." I pointed out that between the Secret Service and the press, this was not only not done by the candidates but not do-able. "We'll find a way." He was confident. "The point is he gets out there among the ordinary people, and he talks straight to them." What, I asked, masking my inner despair with a Mickey Rooney smile left over from Boy Airman days, "does he *say* to them that's going to be so important?" Capra was radiant in his vision. "He quotes Lincoln to them . . ."

I pointed out that Lincoln quotations probably wouldn't win anyone any votes. Certainly, they would not amuse the blacks who were in rebellion that year, 1963. But Capra was exalted. He had also visualized the scene. "Now then, get this. *He dresses up as Abraham Lincoln.* Then he gives them the Gettysburg Address, or something."

I said that I thought that this was truly inspired. Then I went to United Artists and got Capra off the movie and put myself in control. Next I picked a pair of bright young producers to produce, and we hired a director who had worked for me in television.

Henry Fonda played the lead without once resorting to the stove-pipe hat that he had worn with such magical effect in *Young Mr. Lincoln.* Those who would like to know Frank Capra's version of all this will find *his* story in his memoirs. In any event, I was able, that once, to screen our politics the way they are or were as of 1963. The picture was also entirely mine until I got to the Cannes Film Festival to receive a prize and saw, on a billboard, a vast advertisement for *The Best Man—un film de Franklin Schaffner.*

But I had pulled it off once, and that was quite enough I,

mistakenly, thought. I returned contentedly to novel writing. I made Alaska into Duluth; also, Myra into Myron, and back again. I meditated on our history and wondered how best to portray it. I chose a method that has been somewhat controversial, to resort to understatement.

I was aware that I would cause distress among those tenured bureaucrats for whom American history is a profession rather than an art. I also anticipated the problems that I would have in trying to keep to what looked to me to be the main track of our history. As Lincoln is the national god, he is always being kept up-to-date. Although a Unionist, he must be made to seem an Abolitionist, and though a Whig republican he must be made to seem an "of-by-and-for-the-people" democrat. The result has been several tons of badly written history, and a curiously blurred figure on the screen of the national consciousness.

In life, Lincoln wanted to colonize the ex-slaves in Central America. During the 1960s this was not god-like; so a number of Lincoln priests in the universities were able to prove to their satisfaction that he had been not only an Abolitionist but an integrationist. In the god-business, it is Proteus who prevails.

Originally I had planned to write around Lincoln in my chronicles. But then the television magnates asked me to dramatize Lincoln for the small screen. As often happens, by the time that I had done my work no one wanted to screen any American history on television that season. So I incorporated the Lincoln presidency into my long narrative. Despite the success of this particular book, I was told by the head of a network that the American audience is not and never will be interested in the life of Abraham Lincoln or in the Civil War. They want only stories of today.

Eventually, others dramatized my Lincoln book, and the result was popular with public and press. It was also very unpopular with the Lincoln priests, who then put their considerable weight behind a documentary on the Civil War that would down-play Lincoln the unionist and would-be colonizer of the ex-slaves. I have not seen the result, but I am happy that my old friend Shelby Foote has become a star at seventy-three.

Although English imports now fill the cabled air with hundreds of hours devoted to the likes of the dim Duke of Windsor, our history still remains unscreened. Privately, the network programmers say that as history is hardly taught in the public schools, there is not much of an audience for strange stories about long-dead people who write with feathers. There is something in this.

Also perhaps more to the point, we are a sectarian nation and our warring sects can collide at any moment. The black population always got the point to the slave-owning Virginia founding fathers, which means that our history, *properly* screened, is a potential hornet's nest.

I often upset professional keepers of the national myths with the phrase "the agreed-upon facts." I would have thought that this was a reasonably careful way of saying that there are not many facts of any kind that we can ever be sure of, and since endless disputes over this or that detail will bring to a halt *any* description of earlier times, there is almost always a general, often exhausted, consensus that Lincoln, say, appears to be on record as thinking that if slavery is not an evil then nothing is evil, and so he *might* be thought of as an Abolitionist in his heart if not his politics. Naturally, some agreed-upon facts are more agreed-upon than others. But these imprecise consensuses are all that we have. Certainly, the notion that, with sufficient graduate students under a professor's magisterial direction, the actual true story of a life lived long ago can be told is nonsense. Even those lives that occurred entirely in the age of newsprint and television tapes and oral histories can never be more than guessed at. Who tells the truth? Who knows the truth? What is the truth?

The *New York Times* is always regarded as an authoritative primary source. But the *Times* often presents as facts fantasies that no one in good faith could ever accept unless he shares the narrow sectarian worldview of the editors. Since I have been occasionally fictionalized by that paper, I keep them at a distance. My last encounter was typical. The interviewer's opening words to me were, "You hate the American people, don't you?" I said, "No, I hate the *New York Times* and the two are not the same." I then turned to the photographer and his assistant and I got them to sign a statement to the effect that the interviewer, not I, had said that I hated the American people; all in all, a curious thing to pretend that a populist had said, particularly one who had made those same people the subject of his life's work.

But the *New York Times* is a reckless paper when dealing with those who question its values; hence, it is a primary source to be used with caution. Since I have been written about perhaps a bit more than most historians, I am not as impressed as they are by what I see in print, no matter how old and yellow the cutting. Obviously each of us has his prejudices, and no one can ever claim purity in the interpretation of those facts that he has chosen to agree upon. But this does not mean, as I am said to have said and did not say, that history is fiction. I only suggest that much of what we take to be true is often seriously wrong, and the *way* that it is wrong is often more worthy of investigation than the often trivial disagreed-upon facts of the case.

Why nations choose some myths to live by and not others brings us to the great proposition of Alfred North Whitehead: "When you are criticizing the philosophy of an epoch, do not chiefly direct your attention to those intellectual positions which their exponents feel it necessary explicitly to defend. There will be some fundamental assumptions which adherents of all the variant systems within the epoch unconsciously presuppose." In other words, listen for what is *not* said.

About once a decade, at the dark of the moon, someone will timidly note that there is a class system in the United States. Promptly, a booming chorus, rather like the old Don Cossack Choir, then starts to thunder across the land as the employees of the ruling class in the schools and the media chant their denial that such a horror could ever exist in a land where the only discrimination is directed against the poor man who wins a lottery: A bit of class prejudice easily remedied once the capital gains tax is repealed.

Agreed-upon or disagreed-upon facts to one side—significantly, Jefferson liked the wonderful phrase "true facts"—there is another handicap that the custodians of our history labor under. They don't understand politics, yet they write about politicians. Recently, a Hungarian-bred American school teacher strategically installed at Gettysburg took me to task. He was upset that "to the general public, Vidal's is the most influential Lincoln image of our time. It is also the most insidiously ahistorical." I think "ahistorical," in this context, means a lack of footnotes. I also like the way he uses the word "image," as if taking for granted that what matters is the images of things and not their reality. But it is not my alleged errors that disturb him so much as the "cynical, amoral world [the book] creates, with a comfortable Lincoln at its center, is surely the worst literary blow against Lincoln's reputation on record and, to a Watergate-tempered generation, all too acceptable."

I noted the historian's provenance as Stalinist Hungary because the style is that of a defender of a totalitarian regime. Yet, surely, the point to Lincoln, or to any leader of a country such as ours, is that he must deal at all times with corruption of every sort, and if he is not "comfortable" in this line of work he should try something else.

It would be nice, said the Speaker of the House, gazing upon the professors that Jack Kennedy had brought to Washington, if just one of them had ever run for sheriff. The problem here is the general remoteness of the American history departments from the world of politics, as opposed to the world of the National Security State, which has been heavily infiltrated by school teachers who might have served their country better by teaching school rather than destroying, say, Cambodia or even disinforming the *New York Times*.

The actual world of politics may be cynical and amoral to a school teacher in Gettysburg, but what he takes to be cynicism on my part is simply realism. As for amorality, that word is so relative in its meaning and so random in its application that one should be wary of using it at all. Actually, what our governors want screened for the masses are heroic morality tales that will so inspire and distract them that they will surrender their tax money in order to maintain an empire profitable to the few and ruinous for the many.

I would suggest that our icon-dusters ponder the cynicism and amorality *back* of the entire political system, and investigate that, if they dare. But the true nature of any political arrangement is one of Whitehead's illuminating *non*-subjects and any attempt to deal with it causes distress in a society where what ought not to be is not. Even so, despite my tendentious nature, I think that I have been tactful in not imposing my own views where they do not belong. In the case of Lincoln, I look at him from every possible angle and leave the conclusion—if any— to the reader. This is hardly ahistorical, but it is certainly not mythical.

Since George Bush and I were brought up on the same movies and newsreels, I think I can tell what he would *like* to do next, though a country with a collapsing banking system is not exactly the best launching pad for a would-be Trajan. Bush sees himself as avatar to Roosevelt and Churchill. He sees this tiny little island—well, this fairly large country, comprising but a third of a continent—as the center of a world empire where everyone will do what we tell them to do because we're stronger than they are; it is also a lot of fun to order people around, and there may even be some money in it if we can periodically blackmail countries richer than we are. At the time of the Spanish-American war, Mark Twain proposed that we replace our flag with the Jolly Roger. Now here it is again, old Skull and Bones at twilight's last gleaming, snapping in the breeze.

For George Bush it is always 1939, the year of *The Wizard of Oz, Gone with the Wind*, and *Young Mr. Lincoln*. It is the year that Hitler invaded Poland; that Japan was conquering China. It is the year when that magnificent windbag, Churchill, was speaking up for war and that truly amoral and cynical politician, Roosevelt, was trying simultaneously to get us into the war while carefully staying out of the war. This sort of statesmanship deeply puzzles school teachers in Gettysburg, where one is either great and good and always right or not.

Bush sees himself in this heroic line of the great and the good and the right. But the world of the nineties does not resemble, in any way, the thirties. There is no Hitler, no Stalin. There are no regnant ideologies other than our own, which is consumerism. There is no enemy of all that is good in the human race unless it be the United States, or at least that military-industrial-political combine that has locked us all up inside a National Security State and thrown away the key.

Although George Bush does not like to read books, he did say, in the 1988 New Hampshire primary, that the presidency is a lot harder job than any Gore Vidal novel might lead you to believe. I wish it were so in his case. As it is, he will try for further military victories. But if the Germans and the Japanese don't pay our bills, then the last best hope of earth will be obliged, under a new president and perhaps political system, to repair our broken state and forego international piracy of the sort that we are lately prone to. He himself is of no account, and unlucky in his epoch. He may dream of himself as a new Lincoln, standing in the wings, but he is no more than another dim Hoover, presiding over what looks to be a pre-revolutionary time. I suspect that even as I write, there is already a great somber figure, ready to play Lincoln when history gives the cue. I hope we survive him.

What sort of country *is* the United States, and what sort should it be? In the interest of pluralism, every minority is to be cherished. That is a given. But the view of the world that we have inherited is the work of white male capitalists, and is that not a limitation? Of course it is. Many of our Spanish-speaking citizens—or part-time citizens—have no plans to learn English. Is this good or bad? Should they be allowed to vote or not?

I have no answer to this problem other than to point out that in human affairs there are always two great forces at work. One is centrifugal, away from the center. The other is centripetal, a coming together at the center. We see both forces loose in the world today. The nation-state of Lincoln and Bismarck is disliked by most of those people who have been confined to it, as Yugoslavia and the Soviet Union are currently demonstrating.

Even so, I think that a balance can be struck between these two opposing forces. Each tribe should have as much autonomy as it wants. Each tribe should also be encouraged to join with other tribes in larger units, like the European common market, in order to form a more perfect economy and environment. Switzerland is always derided by us because we have so much to learn from the Swiss like the Swiss cantonal system that gives every sort of freedom to four tribes, with four languages and two religions. I have some personal interest in the Swiss arrangement, as my father came from the Alpine province of Romano-Rhaetia, which has produced not only its own minority race and language but has made a serene accommodation with the rest of Switzerland. No, we did not produce the cuckoo clock, but the triple-diphthong yodel is absolutely ours.

I suspect that the United States might study with profit the Swiss arrangement; and then accept the fact that much of the southern tier of our country will be forever Spanish. On the other hand, for a reactionary American like myself—I react against the empire and in favor of the lost republic and its eroding Bill of Rights—it is hard to know how to respond to the new arrivals not only from Latin America but from Asia. Do we *force* freedom upon them? Do we have the right to *order* them to accept the Bill of Rights? Or do we let them set up Confucian conclaves within our borders and do their own thing?

It is usual at this point to mention education. The word is always soothing and suggestive, somewhat, of ketchup, which makes everything look and taste pleasantly the same. But discussions of education in America always center on money. How to get the money from the defense department to the schools? This *is* a problem, of course, but there is a greater problem that no one seems willing to address. What should a school teach? It is plain that what we teach now is of no great use to anyone even if what is taught were well taught. Liberal arts means a smattering of everything and not much of anything, while trade schools are thought undemocratic.

I have never in my life been so bored as I was in the

classrooms at Exeter and at the other schools that I went to. Occasionally a good teacher could lift the gloom and, of course, there was an education to be got at school *outside* the classroom. Even so, it seemed to me as if there was a conspiracy not only to make one learn things that one did not want or need to know but, worse, to refuse to teach the things that one was eager to find out about.

The first question I asked when I got to Exeter was, When do we study the Roman Empire? In Latin class, was the dour response: you will translate Cornelius Nepos. What about the French Revolution? What about it? Then I realized with some despair that we would be taught no history of any kind other than the appropriately named Muzzey's *History of the United States.*

I never got over the shock. At fourteen, I had wanted to find out everything that I could about the whole world and its history; instead, I was subjected to Latin irregular verbs for four years. I felt cheated, and I spent my spare time reading about all the things that I wanted to know about while deliberately refusing to learn anything that the school wanted me to know. I barely graduated. But I got a lot of reading done.

I should like for us to abandon our entire educational system as it is now constituted. *Deliberately* abandon, that is; rather than let it vanish, as it is doing through attrition. I would then begin again.

I would make history the spine of the mandatory twelve years of state-imposed indoctrination. Although, ideally, "reading skills" should be improved, this is not going to happen for the third generation of TV-watchers, as well as computer-masters. Therefore, let us be bold. Let us *screen history.*

In the first grade, I would begin with all the theories—scientific, mythical, religious—of the origins of the cosmos and of man. This always fascinates the very young, with innumerable big bangs and flashes of lightning on the screen. I would then proceed for twelve years to teach—that is, screen—in chronological order, the entire history of the human race, east and west as well as north and south. Along the way mathematics and the sciences would naturally enter the curriculum as they entered our common racial history. The delicate issue of sex would be included as a part of man's growing knowledge of biology and of the development of medicine.

I have always found it curious that the two things a human being must cope with all his life, his body and his money, are never explained to him at school. Few adults ever know where their liver is until too late, and few ever know where their money is—until the Savings and Loan system collapses.

By the last year of high school, the young adult would know pretty much where the human race (as well as his tribe) had been in time and space; and where it now is. So much general knowledge might even inspire him to show interest in where we are going or *could* go. During the twelve years, those of a scientific bent would be encouraged and various additional courses made available to them. Those interested in the arts would be sternly *dis*couraged from pursuing any of the arts. This will save many people from lifelong disappointment while limiting production, in the most Darwinian way, to the born artist who cannot be discouraged. As for the universities, I would promptly fire any teacher who went to work for the National Security State. I would also encourage them to teach the young.

Since future classrooms are bound to show more and more history on film, I think it a good idea to make sure that the greatest art is employed in screening not only Lincoln but Confucius and the Buddha. Yes, I would encourage reading and writing for those so disposed, but the generality will get *their* worldview on screen as they now get everything else. Let us face the shift from linear type to audiovisual the way that our fifth-century BC ancestors were obliged to do in China, India, Persia, Greece, as each culture, simultaneously, shifted from the oral tradition to the written text. Where do I stand in all this? Well, I am a creature of the written word, and I only go to the movies for fun.

Where was *I*, when last referred to in these pages? Oh, yes. Alaska. In an army hospital at Fort Richardson, having been frozen in the Bering Sea, a misadventure which Anaïs Nin was to find hugely symbolic: every writer gets the Louise Colet he deserves.

I had, by then, started a novel, about a ship in a storm in the Bering Sea. After the hospital, I was transferred to the Gulf of Mexico. I was unable to finish this novel until I went to see *Isle of the Dead*, with Boris Karloff. As Boris Karloff first haunted my imagination in *The Mummy*, so Boris Karloff, as a Greek officer on an island at a time of plague, broke, as it were, the ice and I completed my first novel right then and there in Apalachicola, Florida.

I have no idea what it was in the movie that did the trick. But then some things are best left to what the surrealists called the night mind, where it is always noon, beneath the languorous palm trees of my *un*screenable Alaska.

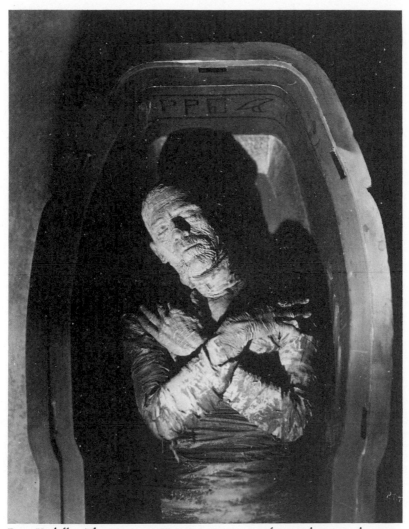

Boris Karloff as The Mummy. *He was present at my first awakening to the movies (1932); and, like a good genius, he presided over the completion of the hard-for-me-to-finish* Williwaw, *thanks to my watching him one night in* Isle of the Dead *at Camp Gordon Johnson, Apalachicola, Florida (1945).*